## PRAISE FOR THE GROUNDBREAKING PARENTING GUIDE,
### *WHAT KIDS REALLY WHAT THAT MONEY CAN'T BUY*

"In a society where too many parents feel pressured to buy their children the latest 'things,' Betsy Taylor and the wise children interviewed here remind us of the essential gifts every child really needs but many children feel they are missing. WHAT KIDS REALLY WANT THAT MONEY CAN'T BUY is a welcome and much-needed resource for parents and adults everywhere."

—Marian Wright Edelman, president, Children's Defense Fund

"Practical solutions and inspiring ideas. . . . The children in this poignant, powerful book speak for all our children, and their message is all too clear: We don't need any more stuff, but we do need to find our way back to our families. Betsy Taylor provides an indispensable road map, leading us to what really matters."

—Katrina Kenison, author of *Mitten Strings for God*

"Many tips and resources to help parents bond with their kids."

—*Riverside Press-Enterprise* (CA)

"Like Rachel Carson in *Silent Spring*, Betsy Taylor's service is to be the messenger for our children. With her keen mind and compassionate spirit, with her incisive social observations and practical tips, she calls us to action. I hope this book, like Carson's, galvanizes our citizens into positive protective actions."

—Mary Pipher, PhD, author of *Reviving Ophelia*

"Throughout her book, Taylor offers tips and suggestions to battle marketing and advertising influences."

—*Washington Post*

# What Kids Really Want That Money Can't Buy

## Tips for Parenting in a Commercial World

## Betsy Taylor

**WARNER BOOKS**

NEW YORK   BOSTON

Warner Books

Time Warner Book Group
1271 Avenue of the Americas, New York, NY 10020
Visit our Web site at www.twbookmark.com.

Printed in the United States of America
Originally published in hardcover by Warner Books
First Trade Edition: December 2004

10 9 8 7 6 5 4 3 2 1

The Library of Congress has cataloged the hardcover edition as follows:

Taylor, Betsy.
    What kids really want that money can't buy : tips for parenting in a commercial world / Betsy Taylor
        p. cm.
    Includes bibliographical references.
    ISBN 0-446-52964-8
    1. Parenting. 2. Children--Life skills guides. 3. Children--Conduct of life. 4. Child consumers--Psychology. 5. Simplicity. 6. Social values. I. Title.

HQ755.8.T36 2003
649'.1--dc21

                                                                    2002033161

ISBN: 0-446-69189-5 (pbk.)

Designed by Meryl Sussman Levavi/Digitext

To my father, Neil,

and in memory of my mother, Anne,

for their boundless love

# Contents

# Acknowledgments

This book would not have been possible without the support of numerous individuals. Thanks to Gina Duffin for proposing that the Center for a New American Dream conduct a contest asking children what they really want that money can't buy. The staff and board of the Center deserve my gratitude, especially for coping with my periodic absences as I toiled with this book while running a growing organization. Several current and former staff members helped with research on kids and commercialism, including Eric Brown, Monique Tilford, Laura Hartman, Sara Pipher, Erin Yost, Katie Milligan, Kathryn Bangs, Erica Morgan, and Trish Wotowiec. Thanks to Megan Scribner, Rebecca Mazur, and Andi Pearl for reading an early version of the manuscript and giving me helpful advice. My executive assistant, Amy Rutledge, served as liaison with Warner Books, helped with research, and provided chocolate in ample quantities to spur me on.

Thanks to my agent, Joann Davis, for helping conceptualize the book and for successfully taking the concept to Jamie Raab at Warner Books. Jamie is a superb publisher and editor and provided critical midcourse corrections. Frances Jalet-Miller, Jamie's gifted associate and fellow editor at Warner Books, gave me tough love and was exceptionally helpful and insightful throughout the final phases of writing and editing. Colleen Kapklein deserves special thanks for helping with the book's development, including invaluable assistance with writing.

I am deeply grateful to the many individuals and charitable foundations that support my work and the programs of the Center for the New American Dream. I owe singular appreciation to Peter Barnes who generously offered me writing retreats at Mesa Refuge and enthusiastically supported the project. Lani Duncan, Carol Hoage, and Karen Woeste helped me stay centered in the midst of it all.

Finally, I want to thank a few very special people who helped shape my ideas and insights about parenting and living consciously in a commercial world. Gordon Cosby is a visionary leader who has inspired, provoked, and taught me a great deal about what really matters in life. Donella Meadows helped me ask the big questions and, though gone from this world, she continues to influence my path. Alan Durning, Ron Heifitz, Juliet Schor, and Mary Pipher are towering thinkers and doers who have given me big "Aha's" about life. Neil, John, David, Uncle Hal, Aunt Barb, Lynne and the Swisher cousins, along with Taylor and May relatives from Delaware to Michigan, have taught me the importance of extended family. My husband, Denny May, a humorous and acerbic critic of consumer culture, has held me to high standards while providing immeasurable support and love. Thanks to Emily and Gus for tolerating my writing and bringing me so much happiness. And finally, I am deeply grateful to my parents, Anne and Neil Taylor, for giving me an early appreciation of life's nonmaterial sources of joy.

# Foreword

by

Mary Pipher, Ph.D.

This book grew out of a contest by my favorite nonprofit organization, the Center for a New American Dream. The Center posed the question, What do you want that money can't buy? Over two thousand young people between the ages of five and seventeen responded with a touching array of stories, essays, and artwork. The responses of these children told us that they want love, respect, more free time, more contact with extended family and the natural world, and a healthier, more peaceful planet.

In a world where advertisers now target the age zero to three demographic group and boast of "cradle-to-grave marketing," there is a poignancy and urgency to kids' requests for simple experiences that humans have always found pleasurable—walks in the woods, stories from grandparents, or chances to snuggle with parents by a fire. It's amazing that kids, who on average see twenty to forty thousand commercials a year, are so wise about what they truly want and need.

Much of what modern kids want I had as a child. But there has been a steady diminishment of opportunities for these experiences over the last century. This is not to say that the quality of parenting has declined. In fact, most modern parents try harder than earlier generations of parents. It's just that the culture we live in has made it harder for good parents to offer their children what they need and want. A simple way to support this statement is to look at four generations of my own family.

My mother grew up on a ranch in eastern Colorado. She and her four siblings worked with horses and cattle from the time they were young children. Information and entertainment came from their small community of Flagler. The family had no exposure to media or advertising. Furthermore, this was during the Dust Bowl era and the Depression, and no one had money to buy anything. In spite of the poverty, my mother had a wonderful childhood. The family worked together, played all kinds of card and board games, read aloud to each other, and sang to the homemade music of a violin and piano. Extended family visited often and stayed a long time. Scottish grandparents lived with the family in their later years. My mother told me hundreds of stories about everything from killing rattlesnakes, to picking up peaches from an overturned boxcar, to the victories of her small town basketball team. She knew everyone in town, and they knew her. Saturday nights the country people shopped, and Main Street was a community party.

My own childhood was only slightly more modern. I grew up in tiny Nebraska towns where I also knew the names of all the people and all the dogs. Relatives sent their kids to live with us over the summers. My father's mother lived nearby. I spent long, lazy summer days reading under trees, exploring creeks, or taming various wild animals I found. Except for church and school, I had no structured activities. If I wanted to see someone, I biked to her house. Our family didn't have a television until I was ten, and even then television was a grainy test pattern many hours a day. Earlier I'd learned to seek my information from people and books, and I never really got hooked on the tube. My exposure to ads was minimal. We ordered our clothes from the spring or fall "Monkey Wards" catalogs. In my schools, we had no Channel One, and in fact, about all we could buy in our little town were groceries, chicken feed, gas, garden seeds, and comic books.

My kids, born in the 1970s, grew up in a town of two hundred thousand people. They saw their grandparents frequently, but had limited time with extended family. They were exposed to the whole catastrophe of modern marketing, media, and technology, but in relatively small measure. They'd been educated to want Cabbage Patch Kids, action heroes, Nikes, and sugary cereals, but generally we could deflect their interests. We had a television, but kept it in the basement, and were mostly too busy with other activities to watch it. Our family had dogs, cats, chickens, and hamsters, and we camped and fished for vacations. But our kids were farther from wild places and had less unstructured time outdoors than I had as a girl. The biggest difference between their childhoods and mine was in the amount of free time. Sara had violin, piano, art, writing, and acting lessons, as well as soccer and softball. Zeke had karate, softball, swim team, and various camps. They couldn't navigate the world on their own. We arranged activities and drove them most places. Their summers were not as lazy as mine. They had less time to lie in the grass and watch the clouds change shape.

Now I have my first granddaughter, Kate, born in 2001. She lives in a quiet college town surrounded by cornfields. She has two sets of grandparents who live in neighboring states and who desperately want to see her, but are busy with full-time jobs. Her parents love the natural world, but they will have to make a real effort to keep Kate connected to it. It's not just outside their front door. The state and national parks are more crowded, and the wild places are less available to families. Kate's been born into a world of Teletubbies and GAP for kids, of Joe Camel and alcoholic drinks that taste like Kool-Aid, and two-hundred-dollar tennis shoes and clothes for young girls that make them look like hookers. She'll grow up surrounded by e-mail, cell phones, Palm Pilots, and video games. She'll have much more access to products, but less access to the things kids want that money can't buy.

A few years ago I wrote a book called *The Shelter of Each Other* about the changes in the cultural landscape for families over the course of the century. I argued that to survive in the modern world families needed to be intentional in their choices. They needed to protect their families from what is harmful and noxious in the culture and connect them to what is good and beautiful. I didn't tell families what these things were. In fact, deciding what is harmful and what is good is the family's job. But I did say that if families were not intentional they would end up stressed, rushed, unhealthy, addicted, and broke. This marvelous book, *What Kids Really Want That Money Can't Buy,* is a continuation of my argument, only this time our children are making the profound points. They are pleading with us to slow down and play with them. They want us to tell them stories and take them to visit their grandparents and cousins. They want family dinners, card games, pets, and meaningful projects. They want more fun and less stuff, which is the Center's motto.

Betsy Taylor's service is to be the messenger for our children. She is carrying their words from the Center's contest into our hearts. With her keen mind and compassionate spirit, with her incisive social observations and practical tips, she calls us to action. Like Rachel Carson in *Silent Spring,* Taylor identifies a toxic force in our culture. For Carson it was DDT; for Taylor it is consumerism with its harmful effects on families, communities, and our planet. Advertisers have tried to turn our children's dreams into shopping goals. Mercifully they haven't succeeded, but this book leaves no doubt that children yearn for many of the things that, in our childhoods, we adults took for granted. Taylor urges us to work together to give kids what they most want. I hope this book, like Carson's, galvanizes our citizens into positive protective actions.

# Part One

# What Kids Really Want That Money Can't Buy

## Chapter 1

# What DO Kids Really Want
# That Money Can't Buy?

*A happy heart.*
—Lydia, 5

"A Happy Heart." Artist: Lydia, age 5

THIS BOOK is for any parent who has been asked—okay, *begged*—for the latest toy, item of clothing, electronic gadget, or junk food. It's for any moms or dads who have spent money they didn't really have to meet their kids' demands, or bought something they didn't really approve of in response to those demands. If you've ever been mind-boggled by the sheer amount of *stuff* in your kids' rooms, or wondered if it is possible to escape the excessive materialism of our times, this book is for you.

Raising kids in today's noisy, fast-paced culture is difficult. Each day, kids are exposed to a barrage of commercial images and messages clamoring to sell them something. The result is a new generation of hyperconsumers growing up right in front of our eyes. For many kids and adults alike, the drumbeat of our times is about never stopping in the race to get ahead—no matter the cost.

Yes, we live in a time of extraordinary opportunities and choices. Yet there are costs to our frenzied focus on acquisition, not all of them monetary. Kids and adults are speeding through life trying to do and get as much as possible. As a result, many young people complain of sleep deprivation, stress, and depression. Commercial pressures also encourage spending rather than saving. In 2001, for the sixth year in a row, more Americans declared bankruptcy than graduated from college. University administrators cite financial mismanagement as a crisis among college students, and the average personal savings rate in the United States has plummeted.

Parents worry that their children define their self-worth through possessions and have little or no ability to delay gratification. One national poll found that 85 percent of parents are worried that their kids are becoming too materialistic. And though we don't think about it too often, creating a whole new generation of superconsumers threatens the environment as well. Americans consume more paper, energy, and aluminum per capita than any other group on earth, and our kids have grown accustomed to our throwaway culture.

When a society is so preoccupied with material things, children and adults lose touch with noncommercial sources of happiness. As noted author and clinical psychologist Mary Pipher, who wrote the introduction to this book, put it, "This generation is the 'I want' generation. They have been educated to entitlement and programmed for discontent. Ads have encouraged this generation to have material expectations they can't fulfill." Many parents want to provide a little shelter from the "more is better" culture and help their kids reconnect to slower rhythms and nonmaterial simple pleasures.

◆ ◆ ◆

I've struggled with these issues myself, both as a mother of two pre-teens, and as director of the Center for a New American Dream, a nonprofit organization that challenges commercialism and helps individuals and institutions consume responsibly. As one of our initiatives, the Center surveyed American parents on their attitudes about kids and commercialism—and found, to no one's surprise, that they are very troubled. Our nationwide poll showed that the vast majority of parents feel their kids are overly materialistic, and many feel they are losing ground in the struggle for the hearts, minds, and wallets of their children. Almost four out of five parents think that marketing puts pressure on kids to buy things that are too expensive, or bad for them.

We all want our kids to be successful and happy, yet it often seems that more stuff is all our kids *do* want. So we decided to ask the kids themselves what they want that money can't buy, by sponsoring an art and essay contest posing that question. The answers we received were moving, powerful, and simple. Our kids do want more than material things. Much more. They want time to enjoy life, and more old-fashioned fun. They want more meaning and purpose and less stress and homework. Kids want respect and friends who will like them for who they really are. Most of all, they are asking for love.

By highlighting what kids really want that money can't buy, this book suggests how to meet your children's deeper wants and needs. To parents from all walks of life, it offers practical tips for raising healthy kids in a commercial world. Most of all, it will help you slow down and rediscover life's simple pleasures with your children.

I must confess right up front that I bought my son a pair of over-priced basketball shoes. Yes, I spent $129 on one pair of shoes—shoes that are at least twice the price of similar quality shoes thanks to the famous name attached. Shoes I knew my son would outgrow in a matter of months!

Still, I bought them. I bought them because my son pushed for them. He wheedled. He asked nicely. He mounted arguments worthy of the best trial lawyers and philosophers. He wore me down.

Does any of this sound familiar? Commissioned by my organization in May 2002, a poll of teenagers showed that the average American twelve- to seventeen-year-old will nag nine times to get a product his or her parent refuses to purchase, and about half the parents give in at the end of all that pestering. Maybe it isn't shoes that capture your kids' attention, but I'm willing to bet that you've had a similar household debate, probably more than once! Your son or daughter may want a cell phone "like everyone else," or "need" expensive low-cut jeans and designer flip-flops. Perhaps you're being lobbied for yet another video game with a parental advisory label for violence. You may be one of those parents who can't make it down the grocery store aisle without hearing cries of "buy this!" every few feet. (Why doesn't this ever happen in the produce aisle?)

Or the symptoms in your house may be subtler. Are you contemplating an elaborate birthday party for your four-year-old, laying down gobs of money for a fancy outing for twenty kids, and then even more money on thematic goody bags? Is your middle-schooler unable to put together one complete outfit without a corporate logo on it? Have you ever worried if you are spending *enough* on a gift for your child to bring to someone else's party? Do you often spend your "family time" at the mall, even if there's nothing in particular you need?

It's almost unavoidable. Ours is a consumer culture. There's tremendous pressure to get, buy, have, and spend, and children are by no means immune to that; in fact, they are the *most* vulnerable to it.

Marketing to children has reached new heights. According to recent marketing industry studies, advertisers are working to get brand loyalty from kids as early as *age two.*

Back to those basketball shoes. My son *loved* them. He wore them every day, took meticulous care of them, played excellent basketball. So I guess there's a happy ending to the anecdote.

But I'm still conflicted. I want my son to be happy. I want his needs to be met. I want him to find common ground with his peers. I want him to pursue what he loves doing. But I also want him to think critically and at least consider my value system, to know the value of money, and what it can and can't do. I don't want him to *need* overpriced shoes. None of the things I wish most fervently for him require any specific brand name.

Those shoes weren't going to make or break our family budget. But they also weren't going to make or break my son's life, or his basketball game either. The problem was, he genuinely felt they would. We could afford them. My son doesn't ask for much, really. We indulged him.

If you've ever done anything like that, you probably identify with the parents interviewed for the Center's poll who were worried about how our commercial culture is affecting their kids. We talked to hundreds of parents nationwide about their struggles with materialism. Almost two thirds said their own children define their self-worth in terms of possessions. More than half reported buying their children a product that they disapproved of because their children wanted it in order to fit in with their friends. Nearly a third admitted they are working longer hours to pay for not-strictly-necessary things their kids nonetheless feel they need. This is an issue that cuts across all geographic areas and all income levels.

Parents place the blame squarely on the shoulders of the advertising and marketing aimed specifically at children. Eighty-seven percent said advertising makes kids too materialistic. Seventy percent feel that marketing hurts children's self-esteem and has a negative effect on their values and worldview.

Parents are right to be worried. Virtually from birth, children are bombarded with TV commercials, banner ads, billboards, product placements, radio ads, corporate logos, and more. Kids have more of their own money to spend than ever before—and advertisers want it. American kids ages four to twelve spent $31.3 billion of their own money in 1999. In 2001 teenagers spent $172 billion. Children also influence an estimated $300 billion that parents spend annually, making them even more attractive to marketers. So companies spend their ad budgets—to the tune of billions a year—to try to get kids to buy, buy, buy and to influence how much and precisely what their parents buy. Chapter 11, Shelter from the Storm, discusses in detail the impact of corporate marketing to children, but for now, it's worth remembering that no child is immune to commercialism. Nearly half of all parents we surveyed reported that their children began asking for brand-name products by age five. Over one in five parents said it started by age three. The children may not know their letters or numbers yet, but they can spot a corporate logo from a mile away.

What do kids make of all this? They've never been shy about telling us what they want to have or buy. We are more than familiar with their desire for money and material goods. But is there something more we are not hearing? What *else* do they want?

As I mentioned earlier, the Center for a New American Dream sponsored a national art and essay contest posing this question to kids under eighteen. What we officially asked is: What do you really want that money can't buy? Besides being greatly impressed by the sheer volume of responses we received (over two thousand), and being touched by how many children were clearly ready to be heard on this subject, I also was deeply moved by the depth and power of their answers. Their pictures and essays made me laugh, cry, and ultimately feel renewed hope for our common future. Perhaps we don't give our children enough credit for their innate wisdom. This book offers you a chance to listen to their voices and, in the process, to get reacquainted with your own heartfelt longings.

The following chapters delve more deeply into what kids want on the themes kids kept coming back to time and again: parents, extended family, free time, friends, the natural world, spirituality, acceptance, health, and making the world a better place. Frequently, the kids shared their pain or anxieties as well. They wrote of feeling trapped by narrow definitions of success—perfect bodies, clothes, performances, games, and test scores. They expressed a desire to transcend the pressure to do whatever it takes to get ahead. In their quest for deeper relationships, they complained of being too busy, managing overloaded schedules, going through the correct motions, and rarely having time to stop the rush of life. Some said this had resulted in depression, escapism, and uncertainty about their self-worth. Yet in the midst of all their worries and hopes, we heard the unifying message that kids want to give and receive love.

Nine-year-old Mary touched on nearly every aspect of what kids said they want in life with this lovely poem:

> *What do I want that money can't buy?*
> *A raindrop, a dewdrop, the fourth of July.*
> *The pride that comes with a job well done,*
> *My name on the honor roll or a medal I've won.*
> *My mom's bedtime stories—whether funny or scary,*
> *A nighttime visit from the generous Tooth Fairy.*
> *Snow days that keep me home from school,*
> *The sand between my toes and the public pool.*
> *Fireflies illuminating a dark summer night,*
> *The prefect autumn day to fly a kite.*
> *Wrestling with my brothers or hugging my dad,*
> *Helping my little sister read makes me feel so glad.*
> *What I really want more than anything, are the*
> *Things that money can't buy,*
> *Like love, laughter, happiness—*
> *and the beauty of a sunset that makes me just sigh.*

The story of my son's shoes crystallizes the challenge of parenting in a commercial culture. We want our kids to be happy and well adjusted, but at the same time we don't want to give in to corrupting commercial influences. What I hope to provide in this book is deeper insight into what kids themselves say they really want from life, along with constructive tips, resources, and ideas for meeting our children's true wants and needs.

The book is divided into two sections. In chapters 1 through 10 I've focused on what kids say they really want that money can't buy. You will read excerpts from many of their essays in these chapters, on the themes they kept coming back to time and again.

The second section, chapters 11 through 13, begins with an analysis of commercial influences on kids and then focuses on more specific strategies for protecting children from advertising. I make many suggestions for helping kids find fun and fulfillment. Each

"World Peace." Artist: Jennifer, age 12

chapter offers tips and resources for further consideration. The book concludes with an invitation to ask yourself the same question: What do *I* really want that money can't buy? As you hear from our nation's young people about what really matters to them, consider what most matters to you. This book doesn't have all the answers, but I hope it helps you find your way in our increasingly commercial world.

# Chapter 2

## You

*I would want my dad to not go to work. I would want daddy to play games with me.*
                                            —Harrison, 5

*I wish I could have a dad that did things with me and under-stands me when I need someone.*
                                            —Katie, 7th grader

ONE OF THE STRONGEST THEMES running through all the responses the Center received to our "What Kids Really Want That Money Can't Buy" contest was this: Your kids want *you*—your time and attention. Happily, parents and kids are reversing recent trends and beginning to spend more time together again. According to a study released in 2001 at the University of Michigan, both working and nonworking parents spent more time with their kids in 1997 than they did in 1981. Many parents are doing everything in their power to make their children the top priority, and this is precisely what kids say they want!

"Mom and Dad." Artist: Grace, age 6

## Just by Their Presence

So many of my friends have parents that work all the time. They are not sure their parents love them, I guess because they are not there. I want to know that I am loved, because my parents are there. Just by their presence, I feel that I am loved.

My parents love me and buy me many things. But what tells me they love me the most is when they listen to me. Things are great, but what I really want is their time. What my friends really want is their parents' time. Maybe go for a walk, and talk. Maybe a bike ride and a lecture talk about money. If you just do stuff together and smile, I will know you love me.

I do things with my mom a lot, but my dad works and sleeps. I

> know we need the money, but I wish he would do more things with me. What I really want is for all parents to just spend time with their kids. America would be a happier country.
>
> —Erika, 14

As much as we love and cherish our kids, it can be difficult to fully express our love and devotion in an age when many of us are definitely in over our heads. We're juggling work, home, community, extended family, and more, and we often feel unable to give our kids enough time.

It wasn't always like this. In fact, things were most likely very different in your own childhood. In asking for *you,* today's kids are picking up on a relatively recent phenomenon: For the past three decades, parents and children have been spending less time with each other. American parents spent 40 percent less time with their kids in 1985 than they did in 1965. For the most part, this time crunch is because parents are working more. During the past decade, parents have become more aware of this dilemma and are often making heroic efforts to be with their children, but the demands of work are powerful.

Americans working outside the home spent 142 hours (three and a half weeks) more per year on the job in 1994 than they did in 1973. A study by the International Labor Organization, an agency of the UN, shows the trend is only getting more entrenched: The average American employee works nearly a full workweek more each year now than he or she would have just ten years ago. Kids lose out when we work too much.

> What I really want that money can't buy is to see my mom and dad more. Most of the time my mom is at work. I only get to see my mom at night. Sometimes she works from 1:00 P.M. to 9:00 P.M. My dad is always at work like my mom, but I get to spend more time with my dad.
>
> —Kyle, 11

Parents are working more for several reasons: financial pressures related to health care, housing, and educational costs, along with workplace norms and rising material expectations that require ever more income. Sometimes parents try to make up for lost time with money or gifts, but kids can see through this approach.

Rachel, a middle school girl, shares her perspective: "What I want that money can't buy is a real father who cares about me . . . a father who cares about his children, who wants to be with them. Someone who enjoys being around me and doesn't try to buy my love."

I haven't met the kid yet who complains about getting too many *things*. But they *are* complaining about the loneliness and emptiness of life without quality family time. As psychologist and author David Walsh, Ph.D., founder of the National Institute on Media and the Family, put it, "We need to spend twice as much time with our kids and half as much money on them." In response, many parents are downshifting, going to reduced workweeks and exploring home-based work. I took a pay cut to have a four-day workweek, and the trade-off of money for time was definitely positive for my family. Hundreds of other families connected to the Center for a New American Dream have taken similar steps.

Of course, most parents don't have this option of reduced work-weeks, and many must work long hours to make ends meet. If you're in this category, you need not despair. Kids can have many of their needs met even if you are often pulled away from home, just so long as they know you *want* to be with them. Katie, thirteen, writes, "you want to have your parents want to spend time with you, even if you act like you don't care. You want them to be around, but even more, you need to know that they want to be with you, even when they can't be. You don't want to feel like a burden to them. What I want is for my parents to tell me they want to be with me, to call me, to check in with me, because then I know they're really thinking about me, even when they're not home."

If you are putting a priority on togetherness, and your children know it, they'll understand your absences as well as your presence. I can't explain it any better than thirteen-year-old Jennifer:

"My mom is divorced, has been for nine years now. She's worked two jobs for nine years and has raised two kids. She has done everything she knows how to do to be a good mother to my brother and me. She has even worked on the weekend just to take a little time off on Fridays to come and see me with the band and some of the football games. My mother is a very intelligent and strong-willed woman. . . . She has never given up on anything that would better our family life. No matter what my brother and I have done wrong, she has always told us that she loves us with all of her heart.

"If I had to think of something that I would want that money could not buy me, I would just want my mother to know that I love her for everything she has ever and will ever do for me. She is the most wonderful woman I have ever or will ever know. I would want her to know that it doesn't matter that she hasn't been there for me as much as I would have liked her to because she was out there doing it for me."

## MISSING IN ACTION

For families with only one parent, or estranged parents, there's an even more serious lack of togetherness. We all know this can be tough on kids. Consider what Cassandra, eleven, had to say:

"My father left my house when I was just two years old, and I have never been the same since. Even though my mom is great and tries to do all she can for me, I still feel the emptiness of not having a dad. I know what it means to long to hear him call my name and to lift me up on his back. I miss his laugh and his strong hands helping me and my mom. I miss him so much.

"I don't think he realizes how much I really need him in my life, and how much he means to me. What I really want that money can't buy is for my father to come back home, or come to see me, or just write me. That would mean more than anything in the world to me. I know some kids are writing for world peace and good things like that, and what I want may seem selfish, but it is the truth. I really miss my father."

I hope her words will reach out to absentee parents and inspire them to bridge the gap. But I also hope Cassandra's words will touch parents living with their children—who too often are not really "there."

It isn't just children of divorce who miss their father's laugh, or a piggyback ride from mom. The contest also drew many responses from kids longing for parents who had died. Seven-year-old Natalie wrote that what she really wants that money can't buy is "My dad. My dad died about four years ago. I would do anything for him to be here with me and my brother and sister. He died in the Value Jet plane crash. He was the nicest dad in the world. We used to play all the time together. He was A Great DAD!"

Monica drew the picture on page 18, of a father she's never met.

We can't replace lost loved ones, but I hope these children's voices will remind all of us to savor our families and make each day count. We can all learn from the wisdom of those who have faced the death of parents too early in life, children like Natasha, sixteen, whose mother died of cancer:

"Sometimes at night I pray for a 'Fairy Godmother,' and if she would really come to me one day I would wish for at least one more day with my mom, the way she used to be, beautiful in and out and the best mother in the world, and I would tell her how much she means to me and how much I love her, and I would thank her for always being there for me and everything she's done for me. Seeing my mother again and telling her the things I always wanted to say but never did is something money can't buy me, but the one thing I want most!"

Jenny, sixteen, wrote on behalf of her stepbrother, Tice, whose father, Bobby, was killed by a drunk driver when Tice was only two: "Tice, my brother, is left with only a vague memory of his father. Tice will never truly understand the love his father had for him. Witnessing how the loss affects this young child makes my heart ache with every single beat. The experience of the father-son picnic will never be known to this innocent child. The fatherly advice about girls, drugs, school, driving, work, and so much more will never be presented to Tice. Tice has been deprived of something so special and important to any human. If there were only one thing I could obtain that money could not buy, I would choose Bobby's life."

We need to take time with our children today. Don't wait for tomorrow. Tell them how you feel about them, offer a hug, do some-

"My Dad." Artist: Monica

thing that lets them know how much you love them. We all know that life is short. Our children will be sustained throughout their lives by the experiences and memories we create together now.

## MAKING THE CHANGE

Lack of time together affects all families. Whether you're single, married to another working parent, or in a household with a full-time parent at home, you probably struggle with overscheduled lives and want more "down time" with your children. But how do you achieve that? The key step is simply recommitting to spending more positive time with your kids. By taking a good look at your lifestyle and work options, you can make a lasting difference in your family's life.

Knowing your core priorities is critical. Ask yourself, How much is enough? Americans from all backgrounds are buying upward, upgrading their lifestyles, taking on more debt, and in the process often unintentionally putting the squeeze on family time. Sometimes we may unwittingly opt for more and bigger vehicles, appliances, and even homes and then find ourselves locked into debt payments and work schedules that keep us from enjoying simple pleasures with our kids. Ask yourself about these trade-offs and then make your lifestyle decisions.

Examine your work options. Is it possible for one parent to work a reduced workweek, or to negotiate more family-friendly working hours, allowing one parent to be home after school, for example? Not every job will allow for flexibility, but you also aren't going to get any leeway unless you ask for it.

Check out your child's schedule too when you try to regain some time together. Sometimes you have the time, but they don't! As you look at your own priorities, you need to consider your children's as well. If encouraging your kids to do more, such as playing "up" in sports or building their precollegiate résumés with extra activities, takes them away from the family most evenings and weekends, you may need to rethink the agenda. Curiously, this pressure for kids to constantly prepare for the future rather than enjoy life now may stem from the same fears that propel their parents to work so hard. Sometimes resisting the need to have your kid always be ahead can be the ticket to greater and more lasting happiness now, and can lead to deeper contentment throughout your child's life.

## COMMIT TO TIME TOGETHER

We need to be conscious about setting aside time to be together. What's worth more than time with our kids? The time we spend together does-n't necessarily have to be extensive or spent in any particularly special way. In expressing her heart's desire, Noe wished for "spending time with your cool family," and she drew it in this family portrait.

"... spending time with your cool family." Artist: Noe

A second grader named Karen asked only for "kisses from my mother." Camie, fifteen, explained it this way: "When I was younger, it was just my mother, sister, and me. My mother worked three jobs to keep us afloat. . . . When we didn't have any extra money, my mother, sister, and I would pretend to have a picnic in the living room, like we were camping. Mama would pack real picnic food, put it in a basket, and round up Joanne and me. We would eat and laugh about the littlest things.

"Now I live very comfortably, and when I want something, I get it . . . but I am not happier. . . . Even with all the money in the world, true happiness can't be bought."

Seth, eleven, is also tuned in to the simplicity and power of parents and children just being together: "Money could never buy the conversation that my Dad and I have in the car on the way to hockey practice. We talk about everything that you could think of. We talk about friends and about what is going on in the world. Sometimes we talk about music, but most importantly, we talk about life. What is going to happen, what not to do and what to do. I love the time with my Dad, and no one or no thing could replace it."

What exactly works will be different for different families, but rest assured, you don't have to do anything fancy. All you need is regular and reliable time together, and to be fully present in whatever time you do have. Authentic, focused, sincere togetherness is what kids crave. Fourteen-year-old Lizzie said, "just being in the same room—maybe reading or resting—feels good. We don't have to be doing anything to have that warm feeling of togetherness." The idea is to have time together that you and your kids can count on, no matter what. For the days, or stretches of days, when time gets really tight, the regular routine of protected times provides a safety net. When you must work long hours, as long as you communicate and share your love along the way, your children will know you're doing it for them.

Even in the rush of everyday life, there are always ways for parents and children to have time together. Here are some ideas to get you started in carving out some extra time with your children.

## Create Kid-Centered Routines

Try to have at least one small part of your day focused exclusively on your kids. It might be a morning walk to the bus stop or coming together as a family at dinnertime (turning off the television and ignoring the phone). You might devote ten minutes exclusively to being together at the end of the day for "tuck in," or chat together each night while doing dishes. Sometimes these relaxed moments are when kids really open up and share what's going on in their lives away from home.

## Make Vacations Count

Take your vacation time every year, even if you aren't traveling anywhere in particular. When you do go, leave work behind. An Anderson Consulting survey showed that 83 percent of U.S. workers on vacation kept in contact with the office. An American Management Association poll revealed that more than one in four vacationing managers are in *daily* contact with the office, and 37 percent call in every two to three days. A working vacation is not a vacation, and I'm betting your children want you off the cell phone and on the beach with them.

You don't have to visit ten European capitals in two weeks or be pampered at a Caribbean resort to make an amazing family vacation. As long as you are not working, you and your kids can connect and, for a period of time, completely stop worrying about the past or the future and simply savor the present moment. Visit different playgrounds in your area, attend a free outdoor concert, or stay up late with popcorn and home movies. Check out local options for free ball games or entertainment. Don't let a single year rush by without setting aside some days for these priceless times of retreat and rest.

## Play Hooky

Once or twice a year, take a day off work and school (or perhaps a day off work when school is closed for teacher conferences) to spend time together. Use it to do something unpredictable and memorable. Ride bikes together. See a play. Visit a museum or rent a canoe. Follow your children's passions. If they say all they want to do is watch a video, just take them off for an adventure anyway. Their initial resistance, in part a consequence of habit, will usually be overtaken by their reawakened pleasure in fun pastimes, and you'll all come home laughing.

## Play

Sometimes life can feel like one highly scheduled, nonstop event. In the midst of school, homework, and extracurricular activities, set aside some time for fun. Dance. Make a collage. Break out a board game or cards. Do the crossword or the word search in the newspaper. Cook a meal together, sing, or play a game of catch outside. Often it's these shared simple experiences that create the happiest and most enduring memories.

## A MORE KID-FRIENDLY SYSTEM

It will never be a perfect system. No doubt, our nation would benefit from some adaptation of the European model—particularly less extended workdays and more vacation time. A growing number of organizations, including the Center for a New American Dream, are calling for a four-day workweek and flexible work options. In the long run, people need to feel materially and personally secure without having to sacrifice so much family time. In our current system, individual households must fend largely for themselves without the support systems that would take pressure off everyone. To put this in context: Among eighteen advanced industrial nations, the United States alone does not provide its citizens with universal health coverage, family allowances, or paid parental leaves. Family-friendly economic policies, such as affordable health care, child care, and housing, along with tax breaks for college savings and retirement plans, would help alleviate the pressure many parents feel to earn money (and work long hours) to meet these core family needs. We could structure things differently if we decided to really make families a priority.

## TAKE GOOD CARE OF YOURSELF

In the midst of all this, you need to be sure to take care of yourself. You can't be present for your kids if you are exhausted from trying to do too much. Every spare moment you have does not have to go to the kids. In our fast-paced world, we must nurture ourselves. This means building in time for exercise, moments of serenity, and friendships. It means indulging now and then in a massage or a weekend away with your spouse. By modeling this kind of balanced living, you are being the healthy role model your children need. And in the long run, this will help your children find their own peace and equilibrium.

As parents, we want so much for our children, and we ask so much of ourselves. In the end, what will most matter to our kids? I think my mother knew the answer. Although she died of leukemia almost twelve years ago, she is still with me. I can still feel her hug and see her smile, and I am comforted by her memory. She made me feel safe, even in the rocky times. She held me to high standards, for which I am ever grateful. I can still feel the warmth of her presence just by closing my eyes. I have memories of singing together, making blueberry pies, talking, playing games, reading together, planting pansies, organizing parties, and later of sharing hopes for the future, debating politics, and discussing marriage. I miss her immeasurably, yet the knowledge of her deep love is always with me. She loved me absolutely, and I knew it. I think this is what our children need most, and we can all be thankful that it is also something every parent can give.

## FOR FURTHER READING

*The Runaway Bunny,* Margaret Wise Brown. New York, HarperCollins, 1991, ©1942.
(A terrific read-aloud book for young children with a core message about parental love.)

*Working Fathers: New Strategies for Balancing Work and Family,* James Levine and Todd Pittinsky. Reading, MA, Addison Wesley, 1997.
(A helpful resource for working fathers who yearn for more time with their children.)

*Parenting by Heart: How to Stay Connected to Your Child in a Disconnected World,* Ron Taffel, Ph.D., with Melinda Blau. Cambridge, MA, Perseus Publishing, 2002.
(A real-world guide to keeping your relationships with your kids on track.)

## Chapter 3

---

# Family

*What I want that money can't buy is for my relatives to live closer to me. My Gran and Papa and my cousins live in Birmingham, Alabama. My other grandma and grandpa live in Raleigh, North Carolina. If they lived closer to me, we would have family dinners. . . . Or all the kids might do a play and the adults would watch. Or my cousin and I might play our guitars together and everybody else would listen. Or we might read together. . . . Well, I guess what I am trying to tell you is that we would have a great time together.*

*—Beth, 8*

ROBERT FROST ONCE WROTE, "Home is the place where, when you have to go there, they have to take you in." In our individualistic and competitive society, kids need and want the ties of kinship. The love and acceptance of relatives is a welcome antidote to the pressures kids often feel to gain self-esteem through material goods or through efforts to impress others. Families, despite their ups and downs, offer unconditional acceptance. Sometimes kids just need the shelter of an uncle's hug, a grandmother's support, or a cousin's constant friendship.

"$ Can't Buy A Forever Family." Artist: Maria, age 16

Kids are longing for an extended family network that is not always easy to come by. The average American moves twelve times in a lifetime, and forty-three million people, including thirteen million children under nineteen, move each year, according to the Mayflower moving company. Many families are fractured by time and distance. According to the AARP, more than one in ten grandparents say they have little contact with a grandchild. Still, according to a recent Gallup poll, 48 percent of Americans say family is "extremely important" in their daily lives—and another 48 percent say it is "very important." Those numbers are even higher for those with children under eighteen, with 60 percent saying family is "extremely important."

Extended families provide a feeling of permanence, a sense of history, support in hard times, and company in good. The bonds of family stand no matter what. You don't even have to like each other to love each other.

In a world that is so often unsettled, where change is rapid and friendships are sometimes transitory, the bonds of family and extended family are more important and powerful than ever. They may be harder to hold on to today, but that makes them even more precious.

Kids no longer live the vision eight-year-old Beth described at the beginning of this chapter. If what she wants sounds old-fashioned, that's because it is the way things used to be, before we all became so mobile. Many of us miss that tapestry of connection, and perhaps children most acutely. The essays and art we received in the contest came back to this territory again and again—kids yearning for relatives who live far away but are close in their hearts. Parental love has a central place in children's lives and takes top prize when it comes to what kids really want that money can't buy. But a close contender is family in a broader sense, starting with siblings and reaching outward to aunts, uncles, cousins, grandparents, and even great-grandparents.

## I Remember Most . . . the Times We Spent Together

When my great-grandmother moved in with us, I was seven years old. She was a big key ingredient to who I am today; she taught me a lot of what I know. . . . My great-grandmother really brought my family together. She added something to it that no one else could have. She was very loving but strict! She would not accept or tolerate any fighting or quarreling that could be prevented by talking. She loved everyone and everyone loved her! It was hard to find something to dislike about her. She was great!

There are many things that I remember about my great-grandmother, but the things that I remember most were the times that we spent together, just her and I. Those were some of the happiest times we had. I remember playing cards with her on the hot summer days; I remember coming home from school and watching a TV show with her in her room. I remember painting her nails two times, maybe three times a week. I remember her voice when she used to speak to me so maturely. I remember the way she used to look at me like I was an angel. I remember the clothes she wore, the way she smelled. I remember the way that she used to hug me in the morning and fill me with love. I remember the way that I could feel her love surrounding me all day and every day. Most of all, I remember the way she loved me. Every time I remember one thing about her, I remember two more. She was such an influential person in my life, and I miss her.

—Sally, 8th grader

## A LESS COMPLICATED LOVE

Love is often considerably less complicated among extended family than it is among those you live with. Grandparents, aunts, and uncles can each play a unique role in kids' lives. They can offer guidance, support, and total love. Without the day-to-day responsibilities of child-raising, these adult relatives are often freed up to simply have a pleasant relationship with their grandchildren, nieces, or nephews. Kids, especially teenagers, may find it easier to deal with these older relatives than with their parents in some instances.

## COUSINS

Cousins also hold a special place in the hearts of most children. With cousins, kids get all the advantages of siblings without having to share parental attention. Cousins bring most of the advantages of friends, with the assurance that the relationship will last no matter what: You're related. You can hang out with a wide variety of ages. You can try out different roles: guide, nurturer, teacher, joker, teaser, flirt, and more. You can share common interests and learn to appreciate others you might never otherwise have been exposed to. No wonder so many kids wrote about missing those who were far away.

### I Want to Be with All of My Family

I was born in Russia and now I live in Jersey City, New Jersey, with my mom. What do I really want that money can't buy? . . . I want to be with all of my family—my grandma, my grandpa, my aunt Aliona, and my aunt Sveta, my little cousins Eugene and Vera.
—Anastasia, 10

I want my country [Kosovo] to be Independent and not to have any more fighting. Someday, if the fighting stops, maybe I will go home again. Then I will see my friends, grandparents, cousins, and others. I miss them too much.
—Armend, 11

## SISTERS AND BROTHERS

Many entries talked about siblings—wanting one, wanting another one, wanting a nicer one! As different as siblings can be, no one else will ever understand you—and the world that shaped you—the same way a brother or sister can. They come as close as anyone can to sharing your childhood experience. They quite literally know where you are coming from. For a lot of kids, this is the first peer relationship.

Lindsay explained all this really well: "I wish my brother didn't have to go away to college. I will hardly ever get to see him after he moves out. . . . Then what? . . . Then what would become of a relationship between lifelong siblings? Siblings are the only people you have your past and future with. Siblings can never be replaced, no matter what you do. I hope me and my brother stay friends forever. It would be a great loss to live my life without him, and I'm not sure how I could possibly fill that void in my life."

It isn't always easy *being* a brother or sister, however, as Shannon, a sixth grader, explained: "What I really want that money can't buy is a sister. I have two older, mean brothers, so I need a sister. . . . I am the youngest and the only girl. I want a younger sister so she can be just like me. . . . I want her to follow in my footsteps. . . . I feel left out when my brothers are having fun. . . . You may not think you are lucky having a sister, but you are."

Siblings are often the best playmates. Jeff, nine, wished for more brothers "so that I can play football. Because then I can set teams up and the names of the teams would be the 49ers and the Green Bay Packers. Because we already have real football helmets. I already have one brother, so now I just need two more."

Siblings can also be soul mates. Harshi, sixteen, described (and drew) a very close relationship to a younger brother: "When my brother was born, I never realized what a gift I was holding in my hand. His name is Amil—which I named him, because it means 'Alive.' You see, he was born premature with many complications, and my family was scared he wouldn't make it. But he did—and oh what a difference it has been to me. . . .

"My brother . . . is . . . someone special in my life. He . . . inspires me to do my best at everything. This is because a long time ago we promised each other that we were going to make the most of our lives and be a SOMEBODY! At that time we were living in a

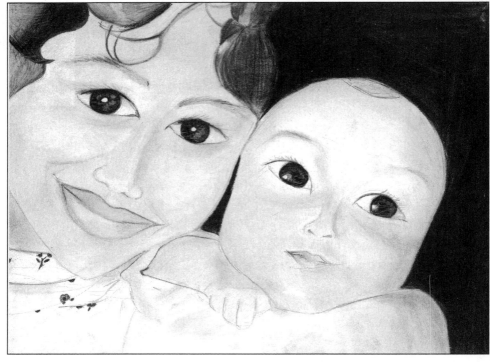

"The day my brother was born." Artist: Harshi, age 16

shelter and eating at soup kitchens. Now we are much better off—in a house we will own soon. But the dreams we made are still the same. And I am proud to say we are well on our way to reaching our goals. Amil is at the top of his third grade class and reads and does math at a fifth grade level. And I, well, I'm not exactly at the top of my class, but I'm in the National Honors Society and am at the top 10 percent of my class. And this year I went to the state tournament for track—Amil and I practiced every day on the track field. We plan to run the Crim race in Flint, Michigan, together! You see, we inspire and motivate each other. And though we argue at times, we are truly the best of friends. So what I want that money cannot buy is for everyone to be loved and needed as I am."

## LONGING FOR AN ABSENT FAMILY MEMBER

We received many contest entries expressing longing for family members who had died. We cannot return loved ones to life, but we can keep the memories of good times alive. Sometimes these early bonds sustain kids in ways we don't fully comprehend. Cristina, who is eleven, wrote about her grandfather:

"I really miss my grandpa. This is what I really want that money can't buy, to bring [him] back to life. . . . I spent lots of fun times with him when we lived in Mexico. I remember that we used to make breakfast together; we would put lots of salt in it and my aunt would get mad because salt is bad for us. I never liked eggs before, but when he would make them, I liked them. I used to go with him to the farm and help him water the trees and flowers. We would try to reach apples and oranges. There was a place where there was a big hole with water, and we used to look for fish, but they would always hide in the dark.

"My grandpa was great. When I was seven, he broke his leg . . . he was eighty-seven. He couldn't go anywhere. Almost every weekend we went to visit him, and we laughed a lot. He had to go to the hospital quite a few times, and my mom and I were the ones who took him. Sometimes we took him with us to our house. . . ."

Ten-year-old Douglas, too, recalled his grandfather:

"I would like to have my grandpa back. He died from a heart attack when I was only seven years old. I would have liked to spend more time with him. He taught me how to play football, baseball, and he came to all my games and practices. He loved me very much, and I loved him very much. He also spent a lot of time with me taking me to lunches, dinners, and ice cream, and we talked a lot about baseball games and life."

Equally heartrending was the entry from Sarah, ten:

"I wish my brother was still alive. I wish that because it would be more fun. . . . He would swim with me and go tubing and tell me that I am a chicken because I go slow on the tube. . . . He would teach me how to build stuff out of wood. We would have built a fort up in the woods so we could run up there when my parents would get mad at us. We would get in fights like all brothers and sisters do. We would be able to tell funny stories to our friends. When we would want to go to the movies or something instead of just me begging we would both beg and my mom would give in easier. On vacation we would have to share a bed and fight over who gets the side closer to the TV. I would always have a friend that has been through the same troubles in school . . . or just talking about something that you don't feel like talking about with your parents. Last but not least, we would be able to play things that *two* people can play. This is what I wish for. My brother was taken away from me when I was two. He died in a car accident when he was four. Now I am an only child wishing I had my brother back."

These children's words can inspire us to take a look at our own families to make sure we are doing all we can to make every day count.

## MAKING EXTENDED FAMILY A PRIORITY

It is hard to maintain relationships if you don't actually get together from time to time. Nurture relationships between your kids and their special relatives by helping them stay in touch. Phone calls, letters, and e-mail can help fill in the gaps between face-to-face visits.

Go out of your way to get relatives together—and to make these gatherings memorable. You don't need to spend a lot of money or make overly elaborate preparations to create some spectacular family experiences. Aligning everyone's schedules is usually the toughest challenge. Splurge if you want to, but remember that simple gatherings, such as picnics, softball games, or reunions held at a local or state park, can be deeply satisfying. Jason, thirteen, is already aware of what those times mean to him:

"With my family, I remember all the fun and good times we have together. Whether it was going to amusement parks and water parks, going to parties, or visiting family members and catching up on some things together, we would always have fun. Good times with your family are what money can't buy that I would love to have with me in my life all the time. Good times with your family are what really keep your family together, besides love, in my opinion. . . . I can remember all the fun things that I have done with my family, and those are memories that I will keep with me throughout my life."

Every family will be different in what they want to do and can do. And of course, plenty of families have serious problems—old rivalries, emotional damage, personality conflicts, and more. In fact, *all* families have their problems. When the problems are just too intractable, or the wounds too deep, try not to let one or two strained or estranged relationships tear up the entire web. Family is family even when there are "issues."

If you've been out of touch for a while, or just want to reinforce the bond, here are a few simple ideas to help you reconnect with grandparents, cousins, aunts, and uncles:

- Organize a reunion jointly with another relative.
- Invite all young cousins to go on a camping trip or see if one wing of your family would like to share vacation time.
- Welcome cousins into your home and do child swaps, giving parents weekends alone now and then.
- Take inspiration from Diana, a mom in Arizona who wrote to the Center about how her family is getting together more often: "This year, instead of buying our dear uncles and grandma more things they won't use [at holiday time], we're using the money to visit more often. We visited in July and October, and will visit again in June, and even possibly in the spring. We get together, make a simple meal, go on walks, play games, or just talk. We have wonderful times! And that's what I want my daughters to remember: fun, simple times of connecting, laughing, and sharing. During the holidays and year-round."

Whatever you do, make it festive and make it fun. If your kids get all excited in the days leading up to the event, and you all enjoy each other's company during it, you'll know you are doing it right. The memories will last a lifetime. Extended family relationships sealed this way will provide your children with a sense of permanent safety and connection in a world that is too often turbulent and unpredictable.

## FAMILY FUN

There are as many ways to knit tight family bonds as there are families. A key is setting aside time to get together and to stay in touch. But there are other ways to cement and hold on to these special relationships. Here are just a few simple ideas:

### Construct a Family Tree

This can be as simple or in-depth as you and your kids want to make it. How much do you really know about your family history? Who were your ancestors? What did they do? What kind of people were they? Start by strolling down memory lane with grandparents, great aunts and uncles, or other older family members. Check books and web sites to help you continue your journey. Check with other distant family members who may have done some research already. Look at local histories and family histories, papers, photo albums, and scrapbooks for clues.

Tobara, age twelve, wrote nostalgically of family photo albums lost in a flood:

The thing that I want that money can't buy is memories. Sometimes I wish I could remember everything about when I was younger (I know that will never happen). One thing that helps you remember the memories are pictures, but that was taken away from me a few years ago. I used to live in a basement apartment, and a few years ago there was a flood. All of the eight photo albums were on the bookshelf on the bottom row, and they were all destroyed by the water. Now, the only baby picture that I have is the one my grandmother has hanging on her wall. Money can never replace the pictures that captured the memories because they were all destroyed including the negatives. No money in the world can replace those wonderful memories.

The Internet is an invaluable genealogic tool; you can get access at your local library if you don't have it at home. The librarians should be able to give you some tips on where to start looking. The web site www.genealogy.com is good for beginners and old pros alike, with tips for recording oral histories, recommended reading lists, and lots of links. When you and your kids have gathered your research, draft a family tree with notes on various ancestors or just chat about what you find with family members.

For more detailed help, you may want to consult *The Complete Idiot's Guide to Genealogy* by Christine Rose and Kay Germain Inglass, or *Unpuzzling Your Past: A Complete Guide to Genealogy* by Emily Anne Croom, which includes how to use family, state, local, and federal resources.

## Tape Interviews

Don't let the great stories get lost to history. Get them on tape! Ask older relatives about their great-grandparents. Children of all ages can enjoy exploring what life was like just fifty or seventy years ago. Encourage your teenager to interview and tape the oldest member of your family. My mother and I once traveled together to tape her aunt, who was turning ninety-five years old. I learned so much during our time together and enjoyed watching my mother's reactions as much as my own. What was it like to live through the Depression, World War II, or the civil rights movement? How did they spend free time before televisions were invented? Is there someone who remembers relatives coming to America as first-generation immigrants? Explore and tape stories of unlikely marriages, unexpected births, eccentric ancestors, and more. This kind of tape can also make a perfect noncommercial gift for the holidays!

## Tell Stories

Kids can get a better sense of their place in the larger world by knowing their own family's legacies, stories, and lore. The stories may be about ancestors way back in the family tree—or tales from your own childhood. They might be about momentous times in history or the minutiae of everyday life, hard times, or accomplishments. Your parents and siblings no doubt have plenty of stories about you—often the most embarrassing ones—which your kids will relish! They'll have a supply of stories about your kids too, which you may be surprised to find are different from your stock. All kids love to hear about themselves, and every telling also underlines just how special that child is to the teller.

## Use School Projects

Incorporate extended family into school projects. Once my son had to interview a former smoker and chose his grandfather. My dad enjoyed it at least as much as my son; he was glad to help, be included, and offer the benefit of his experiences. And my son got to know his grandfather a bit better. Maybe your child can take advantage of her aunt's entomology expertise when science project time roles around, or his cousin's sewing machine when a costume is needed for the school play, or her grandmother's stories when doing an oral history project.

## Celebrate Special Events

Special anniversaries and events often pull families together: a fiftieth wedding anniversary, seventy-fifth birthday, bar mitzvah, or the birth of a new baby. When we attend to these special times, we are sharing in a long-standing part of human history. People have always stopped to celebrate, honor, and pay tribute. It's part of what keeps life meaningful. It helps us receive and express love—something kids clearly want more of.

## TIES THAT BIND

Kinship has been on the decline for over a century now. This means we have to be intentional about holding on to these important ties. Families today are fractured and dispersed. Few live in easy driving distance of one another, and far too often they lose touch simply due to lack of time. Cousins take different paths. Parents separate and remarry. One particular relative may be annoying or beyond reconciliation and so the family just doesn't gather anymore. A few people guard the family lineage and a few others remember the old legends, but many begin to lose touch with the family network. Kids want and need family. They want the stories, but even more, they want the relationships.

## MEMORIES

I want to leave you with one contest entry that really encapsulates the issues in this chapter. It touches on the universal longing for togetherness and the power of shared experiences with close relatives. We can help meet our children's deepest needs simply by reconnecting with extended family. I think you'll be as touched as I was by the simplicity of the memories twelve-year-old Lena invokes:

> *If I would wish for anything in the whole wide world that money cannot buy, I would wish to live in Russia with my grandpa and grandma in their small cottage, in the outskirts of Moscow. This kind of wish may sound very strange, but it's pretty reasonable.*
> *First of all, my grandmother and grandfather are very inter-*

esting people. My grandpa was once a sailor, and he has a lot of stories waiting to be told, not to mention all the underwater, dried-up creatures hanging in his room. This room may sound creepy, but it's really cool. I remember he had a shark's mouth (with all the teeth still in) and a baby shark canned in a bottle and all sorts of shells. He promised my brother and me that one day he'll take us to the Black Sea and we'll go diving there and I'll get to see all this stuff but alive. Plus, since he's been all over the place, he's got coins from places I've never heard of, and since I love collecting coins, his collection interests me greatly, and one day I hope I can inherit them.

My grandma is a person you'd love spending time with too. She knows all kinds of crafts from sewing to paper folding, and fun never ends when you're around her. She can run barefoot in

"Love in Your Family." Artist: Lindsay Ann, age 9

*snow and is very healthy and athletic so you'll never guess her*
*age because she looks younger than she really is. Anyone can*
*learn a great deal from her. . . .*

*I have good memories of picking mushrooms and berries in*
*the forests and sitting on top of tall haystacks in the fields; these*
*kinds of memories bring back only happy feelings. . . . It's great*
*when you are doing work around the house, picking apples and*
*berries in the garden for some jam, or digging in the soil with*
*your bare hands looking for potatoes that haven't been found*
*yet. . . . There's always the chance of going there on summer*
*vacations once a year, though, but it'll never be the same, even*
*though I'll be happy with whatever I can get even if it's a minute.*
*The greatest things in life are the things that don't come from*
*money.*

## FOR FURTHER READING

*The Shelter of Each Other, Rebuilding Our Families,* Mary Pipher, Ph.D. New
York, Grosset/Putnam, G.P. Putnam's Sons, 1996.
(A must-read for adults struggling to maintain strong family and community
ties while protecting children against the harmful impacts of commercial
culture.)

# Chapter 4

———

# Free Time

*What I want, but I can't buy with money, is to be able to stop time. . . . so I don't grow up so fast. I want to stay a little girl. We have so little time on earth, and it goes by so fast. My generation was in such a hurry to grow up. We hardly got to play.*

—Peggy, 11

*I would like more time. My painting shows an alarm clock with time passing quickly, and it's in front of a "window of opportunity." Looking through the window I show that I would like more time to spend outdoors with family and pets, more time to explore the world itself, more time to play outside . . . skateboard, jump on trampoline, etc., and more time to travel and see some sights. . . . Even though I am only fourteen, I feel like time goes too fast, and I never have enough time to do everything I really like to do.*

—Jenna, 14

IN OUR LAND of plenty, adults and kids alike lack one crucial thing: free time. A third of Americans report feeling constantly rushed and out of control of their lives. Forty-five percent say they have less free

"I would like more TIME." Artist: Jenna, age 14

time than they did in the past—and the same number would be happy to trade a day's pay for a day off. Sixty percent say they want to simplify their lives, and 66 percent say they seek more balance.

Children are in the same time squeeze. Roughly 75 percent of a child's weekday is scheduled with school and structured activities, almost double what it was in 1981, according to the October 1999 issue of *Forecast,* a marketing publication. On average, kids ages three to twelve spend twenty-nine hours a week in school, eight hours more than they did in 1981. Children's leisure time—defined as time left over after sleeping, eating, personal hygiene, and attending school or day care—dropped from 40 percent of the day in 1981 to 25 percent of the day in 1998, according to *Time* magazine. Over and over kids wrote that their lives were hectic and exhausting and that they wanted more time.

Take Amanda, age fifteen, from Tampa, for example: "Time. I hustle and bustle from one place to the next. I never seem to have enough time. Consequently I focus on what needs to be done for my life to basically run, yet I am neglecting the one thing that needs to be done, making sure I am happy. It seems like when I look around at the world, it is all based on how much time there is to get something done. I just want to stop and, well . . . smell the roses. In my life I won't remember the high school projects, every meeting I rushed to, or the endless hours I spent on homework. I'll tell you what I will never forget though: friends, laughter, good conversations, funny stories, smiles, words of encouragement, life lessons, and maybe even a little heartache. These are the things that will mold me as a person, and these are the things I wish I had more time for. I don't want to miss out on making a new friend because I simply don't have time. I don't want to be unavailable to help a friend in need because my schedule is filled with things that won't be important in the long run. I want to read a book, sit on a dock and stare at the water, gaze out over a mountain, talk to someone, or even bake cookies for someone special simply because I have the time."

Kids want more time just to be kids. Annie, fourteen, said, "Time is the most valuable thing in the universe, and I'm finding out that I never have enough of it. I mean time to stand up on a green hillside and shout out to the world, to sit and watch the billowing white clouds fly past on a warm wind, or time to lie in the grass and watch the ladybugs crawl up the strong green stalks. I mean the kind of time that everyone needs to stay sane. But it seems like I'm just squeezing by on auto-pilot."

There are many reasons for this time scarcity. Many kids are overprogrammed and feel pressure to advance to ever higher academic, athletic, or artistic achievement. Electronic entertainment has replaced unstructured leisure time, while a growing number of teenagers hold down jobs while attending school. Finally, working parents often need to keep kids in supervised activities. As parents we must examine and gain control of each of these areas if we want to help our kids experience the wonder of free time they are asking for.

## PLAY VERSUS OVERPROGRAMMING

"Play is the most powerful way a child explores the world and learns about himself," says T. Berry Brazelton, a pediatrician at Harvard Medical School who has written a number of nationally acclaimed books on parenting. Unstructured play encourages independent thinking and allows the young to negotiate their relationships with their peers. The phenomenon of scheduling a "play date" reveals that we've taken even the most spontaneous thing of all—play—and contained it within a specific block on our personal planners.

You don't have to ask the official experts, though. Wayne, nine, could tell you: "The thing that I talk about wanting the most is time. I wish that I had more time in a day to play. I would really like more time to learn about interesting things. When I am doing something fun, I get sad when it's over. If I could have more time when I want, I could make fun things last as long as I wanted them to."

Dorothy Sluss, a professor of early childhood education at East Tennessee State University, said, "We don't value play in our society. It has become a four-letter word." Statistics back her up. Since the 1980s, hundreds of elementary schools have eliminated recess, and parents are enrolling young toddlers in a myriad of "precurricular" activities. Pediatrician and author Ralph Minear studied children who exhibit signs of physical and emotional stress and concluded that many of their problems often stem from being given—or asked to do—too much.

Our children are blessed with a dazzling array of choices and opportunities, and we want them to be able to take advantage of them. All of them. We truly want the best for our children. But it's coming at too great a cost. "We're moving, in a cultural sense, in the direction of having every kid be a star," James Dawson, head of the Professional Children's School in Manhattan, told *Time* magazine. "By doing that, of course, what we really say to kids is that normalcy is below par."

> I wish people would stop rushing around! That's all people do any-more (24/7). That's the theme of the world! Do people ever rest? I, for one, hate rushing around. Some people have gotten divorced because they never see each other. All parents do is rush to work, rush home, rush, rush, rush! When do people relax? It seems like the only people who don't rush are the old people. There's even some-thing such as "Rush Hour." Now that's bad. So what do I want that money can't buy? Something simple, for people to stop rushing so much (It's like a hobby now!).
> —Emma, 12

Sometimes the kids themselves may be asking for all of these activities because they feel pressure from you or from peers to keep up the pace. "Children being pushed too hard may not be able to articulate their feelings, but the signs are there. They become emotionally volatile or complain of aches and pains. They can't sleep. They lose touch with their friends," Jack Wetter, a clinical psychologist in West Los Angeles, told *Time* magazine. Wetter believes the current flood of children being diagnosed with attention deficit disorder may be misleading. Many of these children, he says, "just don't know how to express their frustration. By the time they are 16, many are burned out, antisocial and rebellious."

And no wonder. Listen to fourteen-year-old Brittani describe a typical day (on her summer "vacation," no less): "'Time to get up!' It is 6:15 A.M. when my mom bursts through my bedroom door to wake me up for a three-hour swim practice. I get dressed, grab an Eggo, and hop into the van. After a two-hour practice in the pool and an hour-long run through the neighborhood, I rush to the neighborhood pool where I lifeguard from 10 A.M. to 3 P.M. After five straight hours of working in the scorching sun, I catch a number five and a Mcflurry from the McDonald's drive thru on my way to my second swim work-out of the day. Upon completion of this two-hour killer practice, I am already late for my 6 o'clock driver's ed class. When class is over at 8 P.M., I set off for home where the remains of my family's dinner is left on the table for me. Finally, after dinner and a shower, I climb into bed to say my prayers and get a good night's sleep before I must repeat the same chaotic routine tomorrow. My coach says, 'dedication'; 'insanity,' say my friends; my parents say, 'keep up the good work'; I say I need a break! So, after a full summer of this six-days-a-week routine it should be obvious what I want that money cannot buy. I want all the time in the world! Any time would do: nap time, playtime, quiet time, family time, even time out! I need time to curl up with a good book, play with the little kids next door, go on a picnic, see a movie, go to the mall, or just watch a sunset."

It doesn't have to be like this. Just think how different it might be if fourteen-year-old Amanda's vision of free time with her family came to pass: "One of the many reasons I want more time is just to spend more time with my family. It is hard to spend a lot of time with my family these days because of our busy schedule. Another reason I would like more time is to make the most of my life. . . . Having more time each day could allow me to do a little extra work for my parents. I could help my brother on his homework. Time may just benefit in little ways, but those little ways can add up. More time each day would let me do more things that I would enjoy, like spending time with my friends. . . . Time is precious, and we have to make the most of the time we have."

One of the mothers who contacted the Center for a New American Dream for advice reported feeling dismayed by the pressure on kids to gain a competitive edge in all parts of life. "If you don't get lessons started early, all the other children are ahead, in academics and sports, by middle school," she worried. Although benefits may accrue from this push to stay ahead of the curve, the push also typically eliminates free time. We are left with nonstop busy lives.

By really listening to kids and picking up on nonverbal cues, parents can usually sense when their children need to slow down or just stop. Sometimes it might involve talking a kid out of yet another activity. It may be better for your child *not* to be taking Spanish or ice-skating, if that allows time to rest, relax, hang out, be with friends, spend time with family, or be outdoors.

### Happy Day

I want another day in the week where all you do is have fun with your friends. It would be called "Happy Day" because it would be a rule to be happy all day long. . . . There would be no school. The only places that would be open are places where you could have fun. . . .

Happy Day would be between Friday and Saturday. You could stay out as long as you want because there would be no curfew. You wouldn't have to worry about going to school the next day. I would put it between Friday and Saturday because it would make the weekend longer. Happy Day would also be special because it would be illegal to exclude anybody from the fun. If you did, you wouldn't be allowed to participate in the next Happy Day. . . . It would change a lot of people's lives who aren't very popular because they would have many friends to play with on Happy Day.

—Jeff, 13

### SLEEP

Remember too that kids also need a lot of sleep. According to the National Sleep Foundation, students need nine hours of sleep to be completely energized and ready for school. Only 15 percent of adolescents get the sleep they need. Will Wilkoff, a pediatrician and author of *Is My Child Overtired?* says that about 80 percent of the children in his Maine practice are not getting enough sleep.

Many parents are familiar with the daily struggle of getting everyone out the door and to school on time. It's not surprising that 71 percent of American teenagers polled by the Gallup organization in 2001 said they think it would be a good idea if schools started an hour or two later so that students would be able to get more sleep.

## HOMEWORK

Homework is another major culprit putting the squeeze on kids' time. Back in the 1930s, the American Child Association classified homework as child labor, and New York and Chicago curtailed or banned it outright. Things have changed dramatically and have especially intensified in recent years, in part because of reports that suggest U.S. schoolchildren don't compare favorably to their international peers. As a result, students have been bringing home piles of assignments. The homework battle often pits parents who are fighting for quality time with their kids against educators and others who are trying to ensure that students make the grade. Not surprisingly, more than one child who wrote to us wished for less homework. What *is* surprising is that a lot of knowledgeable grown-ups agree.

According to a University of Michigan study, students spend eight hours more a week in school than kids did twenty years ago, and homework time has nearly doubled. In 1981, six- to nine-year-olds did forty-four minutes a week of homework on average; in 1997, they did more than two hours. Study after study indicates that average daily and weekly homework loads are rising for children of all ages, yet the measurable benefits are questionable at best. John Buell and Etta Kralovec, teachers and authors of *The End of Homework,* argued that "both research and historical experience fail to demonstrate the necessity or efficacy of ever longer hours of homework." They say many students, especially junior high and senior high students, are suffering from the "fatigue factor" from putting in fifty or sixty hours a week of class time and homework time, which may burn them out before they go to college.

There are other negative consequences to the heavy workload imposed early on our children as well. The American Academy of Orthopedic Surgeons reports that thousands of kids have back, neck, and shoulder pain caused by heavy backpacks. And too many kids exhaust themselves working late into the night—and have little or no free time. As Megan, twelve, wrote: "If you are like me, you don't like homework. . . . When you have sports that you want to play, it's not easy to play sports and have to do homework at the same time . . . so that is why I don't want so much homework and that includes tests, too."

Denise Clark Pope, a lecturer at Stanford University and a high school curriculum expert, studied five motivated and successful students through a year of high school and concluded that kids feel stuck in a "grade trap" that pins future success to high grades, test scores, and advanced placement courses. As Pope explained in her book *Doing School,* "these kids are caught in a system where achievement depends more on doing—going through the correct motions—than on learning and engaging with the curriculum." One student summed it up this way: "People don't go to school to learn. They go to get good grades, which brings them to college, which brings them the high-paying job, which brings them to happiness, so they think." The truth is, quantity of work, and homework, does not equal quality of education. Sometimes less really is more.

Take a look at the choices you've made about your child's education to see if there's any modification to be done there, such as limiting the number of advanced courses he takes. Talk to your child's teacher and then, if necessary, to the principal and even the superintendent about appropriate levels of homework. Go armed with the data. Team up with other parents who share your concerns.

There are no set national guidelines for homework, but many parents are asking school systems to review their homework policies. In my son's middle school in Takoma Park, Maryland, parents protested heavy homework loads, and in response, the principal asked teachers to cut back on excess assignments. In northern Virginia, the Arlington school district also assessed homework loads and decided to impose some modest restrictions. "We were sending things home with youngsters that required someone with a graduate degree to help," said Kathleen Grove, assistant superintendent for instruction at Arlington Public Schools. After studying the issue for years, the district set strict rules on homework: Schools are asked to give assignments that students can complete independently, and virtually no high school student is expected to have more than three hours of homework nightly. In the Piscataway Townships of New Jersey, the school board advised teachers to limit homework to no more than thirty minutes nightly in grades one through three, fifty minutes in grades four through five, and seventy-five minutes in grades six through eight. It recommends a two-hour limit in high school and discourages assignments on weekends and holidays. One district schedules no homework or sporting events on a given night to allow for family time.

Homework squeezes family life. All parents want their kids to have a strong education, but they also want to have the time to teach them about their cultural heritage, to pass on important life and household skills, and to simply enjoy daily life. According to a 1998 survey by Public Agenda, nearly 50 percent of parents reported having a serious argument with their children over homework, and 34 percent reported homework as a source of stress and struggle. Parents often feel deep conflict about homework, viewing it as an essential part of their child's future success but also as a burden that robs families of critical free time. The notion that more is always better is under hot debate in communities across the nation.

## WORK

As of 1992, five million kids between the ages of twelve and seventeen had part-time jobs, a third of them for more than twenty hours per week and more than ten weeks per year. A recent survey of fourteen- to seventeen-year-olds found that 34 percent were employed sometime during the year, according to David Johnson and Mark Lino's "Teenagers: Employment and Contributions to Family Spending" from the *Monthly Labor Review Online* 123:9 (September 2000).

Part-time jobs often foster independence, responsibility, and good work habits—but they may also be eating up too much of our kids' free time. Interestingly, teenagers from both low- and high-income families devote their income to personal items such as clothing, cars, food, entertainment, and in some cases, drugs and alcohol, rather than college savings or family expenses, according to *Teenagers: Employment and Money Management* by Peggy Patten. Parents can help kids assess their desire for spending money versus their need for free time and make adjustments as necessary.

## ADULT WORK PATTERNS

Parents' work habits are part of the free-time problem too. The majority of school-age children have both parents in the workforce, so their opportunities and options for free time around the home are limited to the extent that they require organized (supervised) activities. Many after-school programs are terrific, yet the fact remains that they are highly structured and typically fail to provide the real leisure time kids say they need.

If your child really needs more down time and you can't be more flexible with your work hours, don't worry! Families in touch with the Center have invented a variety of strategies for handling similar situations that might inspire you. Some have started after-school co-ops with participating parents taking turns watching three or four kids at a time. This way, children can be in a home after school with a supervising adult, but not feel required to be part of something more structured. Parents save money by avoiding baby-sitting costs while giving their kids more unstructured time with friends. It does mean that one parent has to negotiate unusual work hours, say from 7 A.M. to 3 P.M., for one day each week. Other parents are simply cutting back to spend more time at home, opting to make less money but gain more time in their own lives and for their children. That may not be possible or even desirable for every family, but exploring the possibilities can often lead to new and satisfying arrangements for kids and adults alike.

## DIGITAL DISTRACTIONS

Television, computers, and electronic entertainment absorb a huge portion of our kids' time. Gone are the days when kids raced outside after school. Among children six to seventeen, 86 percent have access to VCRs, 70 percent have video game systems at home (32 percent in their own rooms), 50 percent have TVs in their own rooms, 40 percent have their own portable cassette or CD players, and 35 percent have their own stereo systems, according to 1998 data from Roper Starch Worldwide. According to one study, 32 percent of eleven- to twenty-year-olds spend ten to twenty hours a week online.

Kids, like adults, are becoming more isolated due to computers, video games, television, and other supposedly "interactive" electronic equipment. Interacting with a machine bears little resemblance to the rewards of interacting with other people, and instant messaging cannot replace one-on-one human contact. Machines are changing the experience of childhood itself, supplanting traditional activities such as reading, playing, and outdoor exploration.

While watching TV or surfing web sites does constitute free time, it isn't the kind of free time kids themselves are asking for: the spacious, slow time to just be themselves and be with friends. Stuart Brown, a retired psychiatrist and founder of the Institute for Play, fears that too little old-fashioned play can lead to depression and the loss of "the things that make us human beings."

Complete withdrawal from our electronic world isn't necessary, but moderation will help free up the time kids say they want. Parents have a crucial role to play in limiting time with electronic screens of all kinds. Warning: If your kids are used to unlimited TV and computer time every day, it will take a month or two to get past the struggle. No doubt you're already familiar with the cry "But there's noth-ing to do!" Here are a few suggestions for trying to change direction:

- We all know the most important rule in parenting: Our chil-dren do what we do so we must exhibit the behavior we hope to see in them. The best way to reduce tube time is to watch less yourself. One of my husband's good friends raised two daughters as a single parent. When I asked him about his tele-vision-watching policy, he said the girls were allowed to watch as much as they wished. How much did they end up watch-ing, then? "None," he replied. Why not? "Because I didn't watch any," he said. Discuss your desired approach to televi-sion and computer with your spouse or partner and make sure you're both committed to setting limits. If one parent still sits in front of the tube all evening, limiting screen time for chil-dren becomes nearly impossible.

- Get clear about the limits that are right for your family. Some families allow television only on weekends and even then only for a certain amount of time. Others set a time limit in the evening after homework is finished. Try to assess your family's schedule and make a decision about turning the television and computer off for certain periods of every day.

- Be aware of whether you encourage TV watching or computer games as a strategy for getting your kids out of your hair. If this is the case, you may need to rethink your own time as well as what message you're sending to your kids.

- Discuss the new rules and guidelines with your kids and explain your rationale. This discussion will vary according to the age of your children, but you may need to exhibit "tough love" at first and just hold steady despite the inevitable protests.

- Stick to your decision for at least two months, giving everyone in the family a chance to develop healthier TV and/or com-puter habits.

- Offer positive alternatives to television and computer time. Play catch, make a pie, encourage your child to have a friend over, take a walk, or watch what your child comes up with out of the whining and boredom. Maybe you won't totally love his new fascination with building scooter jumps or her desire to design and sew her own fashion accessories, but when you turn off television, you have to turn on life.
- Get together with other families that limit television and have fun.
- Do not, under any circumstances, put a television in your child's bedroom. If they have one, and you regret it, just tell them that it's got to go. They may hate you for it initially, but years later they'll thank you.

"I would want...more time." Artist: Stephanie R., age 11

Our children receive nonstop messages and images pouring from the television and computer, but there is another kind of information, what author and social critic Bill McKibben calls "missing information." It can only be rediscovered when electronic screens are turned off and we have the time to slow our pace and pay attention to the real world—not the artificial one. McKibben says the noise of the modern world makes it harder to hear, but the natural world's signal is still there, broadcasting around the clock, if we can just help our kids hear it. Ultimately, the trick is helping our kids navigate the good parts of this media revolution while creating some shelter against the powerful media forces that distract our children from deeper, nonmaterial pleasures.

## WHY ARE KIDS IN OVERDRIVE?

It's worth pausing to ask why our kids are being pushed to accelerate ever faster in all fields of endeavor, from algebra to athletics. What's behind the pressure for longer school days and years, for more homework, nonstop extracurricular activities, and the incessant chase to do and achieve more? Is it pressure from the federal government and corporate America to ensure our competitive edge at the international level, economic fear brought on by the continual erosion of our societal safety nets, or a quest for a high standard of living for our kids sometime out in the distant future? No doubt, many children in overdrive are developing extraordinary skills and talents, but is the rhythm of their lives healthy? Why is our society apparently willing to jeopardize the emotional and physical wellbeing of our children by structuring educational and social expectations to value the pursuit of more above all other values? And are our children losing out in the process?

Parents who are weary of the race must begin to ask these fundamental questions if we hope to turn things around. President Nixon predicted years ago that we would all have a four-day workweek and that life in the twenty-first century would be defined by leisure. Instead, our furious desire for productivity leaves adults and kids feeling depleted and yearning for balance and free time. We have taken most of our productivity in the form of increased material goods rather than in leisure. This core issue of minimal free time is taking a toll on all of us, and our children are crying out for change.

A large part of the problem is systemic, and requires concerted action at the broad social and political level. In our homes and families, though, there are things we can do. Consider speaking up at PTA meetings and challenging the prevailing norms regarding increased school hours and homework loads. Consider resisting the dominant system by not always having your child on the fast track. Model a new way of living. Slowing down with your child to savor unstructured time is uncommon in today's culture, but it may be precisely what you and your kids want that money can't buy.

Free time is the prerequisite for many of the things kids say they want that money can't buy: time to experience nature, be with their parents, enjoy extended family, and help make the world a better place. In the midst of our busy lives, perhaps the most radical thing we can do, both for and with our kids, is to simply stop and do nothing from time to time.

Cindy, age fifteen, speaks for many kids in her wish for more time: "Sometimes it's frustrating how fast life passes you by. One day you can be laughing and talking with a friend and the next thing you know you and your friend are going off to different colleges. You didn't even see it coming. Sometimes I just want to stop everything and keep it the way it is for that one moment in time. That one moment when everything is perfect and you forget about all your problems and its just you and your friends. It's that moment right before the bell when everyone is laughing and talking and no one is even thinking about the huge algebra test next period. That moment in time when all that matters is the here and now, that moment of bliss experienced not often enough. Time, that is what I want that money can't buy."

## FOR FURTHER READING

*The Overworked American: The Unexpected Decline of Leisure,* Juliet B. Schor.
New York, Basic Books, a Division of HarperCollins, 1992.
(An incisive analysis of why American adults are working too hard and
missing out on true leisure time.)

*Doing School: How We Are Creating a Generation of Stressed Out, Materialistic,
and Miseducated Students,* Denise Clark Pope. New Haven, Yale University
Press, 2001.
(An insider's view of the elite academic track for five high school students
including thoughtful reflections on how the American educational system
has precollegiate kids in a nonstop race to get ahead.)

*Mitten Strings for God: Reflections for Mothers in a Hurry,* Katrina Kenison.
New York, Warner Books, 2000.
(A collection of stories and reflections to help readers ponder how to slow
down and treasure the important things in the midst of a busy, stress-filled
world.)

# Chapter 5

▬▬▬▬▬▬▬

# Friends

*I want a true friend that sticks with you through thick and thin. A true friend that helps me with my homework. A true friend that doesn't make fun of you. A true friend that plays with you.*
—Brandon, 10

KIDS OF ALL AGES need and want friends. Every child wants someone to share his or her journey, yet forming and maintaining friendships is harder and harder for kids today. Large schools, highly scheduled lives, and even basic security concerns can make it tough to build and keep strong relationships. True friends may be harder to find and keep, but kids want them more than ever.

As parents, we know the importance of friendship, intuitively and from experience. Friends offer companionship and pull us through in tough times. Parents cannot (and should not) orchestrate friendships for children, but we can cultivate these special relationships and provide encouragement along the way. Friends are pivotal in helping a child develop independence and a personal identity apart from the family. As fourteen-year-old Elizabeth put it, "Friends help make you who you are."

The kids in our contest wrote of just wanting someone to talk to,

"Friendship." Artist: Jana, age 13

play with, sit with at lunch, or feel comfortable with. They long for someone to support them when the going gets rough, to really get to know and understand them. Kids need someone other than a parent or grandparent to think they are special. They mention over and over again that they want loyalty. Kids are looking for deep, long-lasting, heart-to-heart connections they know they can count on, no matter what.

Take it from Jennifer, fourteen: "Friendship is the caring, sharing, and trust of another person. You get someone's trust by getting to know them, and you get to know them by spending time with them and going through trials 'of life together. . . . A true friend likes you regardless of your money or popularity. A friend is someone whom you can confide in at all times, and who can counsel and comfort you in times of need. Nothing can ever be purchased which is better than a loyal friend. A friend is always there for you and never lets you down."

Aleah concurs: ". . . right now I'm going to tell you the main thing in life that I would love to have that money could hopefully never buy. I would want a friend, a friend that listens to me all the time and never ignores me. A friend that is kind and gentle and doesn't hurt me ever! A friend that helps me when I'm in need and doesn't make fun of me for my problems. A friend that cares and understands me. A friend that isn't rude to everyone, but kind and thoughtful, and possibly a good student. A friend with imagination, citizenship, and loyalty. A friend that stays next to me and acts like a true friend and not just a friend. A friend that supports me and can always give me a compliment when I need one and make me laugh when I'm sad. . . . A friend like this sure doesn't come around often."

Mark, ten, like most younger kids, has even more basic requirements in a friend: "The thing I want most that money can't buy is a friend. I want a friend because I don't want to feel lonely. I want people to go places with me. I want people to play football, baseball, and basketball with me. I want someone to go swimming with. I want someone to play with. I want someone to walk with. I want someone to run with. I want someone to talk with. . . ."

We also had many contest entries from older children wishing for romantic love; the underlying desire is the same as for true friendship: wanting someone to think you are special. Here's just one example, from seventeen-year-old Esther: "When I was little I used to watch Cinderella and Sleeping Beauty and wish that when I got older I would meet Prince Charming. Of course, we would live happily ever after and he would be amazingly good looking and I would be gorgeous, with beautiful, flowing dresses and glass slippers. Even at seventeen, I still wish for Prince Charming . . . [but now] my Prince

"Happiness, World Peace, Love." Artist: Kyla, age 15

Charming does not have to be the stereotypical tall, dark, and handsome Romeo. Rather, he will be someone who will love me unconditionally. . . . But no matter how badly I want to meet that special someone, I know I have to wait for that day to come because money could never buy the true love and happiness I want to be able to share with someone."

## BEYOND ALPHA MALES AND QUEEN BEE GIRLS

Jennifer and Aleah, along with several other kids, touched on the crucial difference between friendship and popularity. Friendship, for the most part, transcends social status and appearances and is based on a deeper intimacy, respect, and affection. Yet all kids have to build relationships in the context of age-old popularity wars over social rank. This terrain is often the most difficult to negotiate—figuring out where you fit in the group and having a sense of belonging.

Sophia has a wise perspective on the nature of popularity:

Why do the popular people have the advantage? During school, I envied those who wore cool clothes and those who were in the popular crowd. The popular girls would always be the great flirters and always knew exactly what to say to make the boys melt. There were some "nerds" in our school, and always during lunch I would glance at them hoping to see a bunch of friends crowding around, but I would only see them sitting all alone. And then I would glance at the cool crowd, talking and chatting excitedly away while other people would sulk around, feeling misplaced. But then I realized one day that the kids who were not in the "crowd" were actually making the people who act like they are better than the ordinary middle schooler, popular. I knew from that day on, I no longer needed to envy those who seemed to be always in the top, because I had learned that they are no different than us. . . . But I knew at least for one day, every single kid in school would like to feel like they belonged and were popular.

Many kids wrote in about the suffering of kids who don't feel popular and can't find a trustworthy friend. Brittany, twelve, wrote: "What I want that money can't buy is to not be teased anymore. I'm not one of the blonde types, and I wish the stuck-ups would stop being so preoccupied with looking like Barbie. They even started an 'I hate Brittany' club. What I want is a true friend, and I don't care what she looks like as long as she is really really nice and dependable and fun."

Hope, also twelve, is going through a similar situation: "I want people to be kind and accept people who may be 'different.' I don't like it when people are rude to people who may be 'different' from them. . . . I'm not skinny and I don't wear Abercrombie and Fitch. I have braces and I only wear makeup occasionally. If you don't wear all that then you're 'different.'"

Psychologist and child development expert Michael Thompson wrote, in *Best Friends, Worst Enemies,* "the criteria for choosing popular peers hasn't changed much in human history. Boys continue to be valued for traits and achievements that signal success at hunting and fighting against the neighboring cave. Girls are valued for their appearance and their sociability. . . . Is it a coincidence that the biggest, most athletic boys and the most attractive, most social girls are over represented in the popular crowd of virtually every school. . . . Socially powerful, popular girls tend to be the most feminine. Likewise, the least popular children are those who stray from the age-old 'ideals' of their gender."

Kids have always had to struggle with these Darwinian battles, but marketers are making the passage through adolescence harder than ever. Any glance at a teen magazine reveals cover-to-cover ads that amplify the importance of conforming to the alpha male and queen bee girl stereotypes—and a lot of the articles are just as bad: "Snag any guy you want with kick butt shorts!" "Dangerously low . . . low rise jeans" "Get inspired. See your stylist." "Make me over!" "Exude cooler" "Better taste, hotter results" "Hot stuff guys" "He's got the look!" "Feeling stressed out? Give your room a makeover! Shop!" (to give you just a few headlines from ads and feature stories in my daughter's teen magazines).

Kids are bombarded with commercial messages urging them to buy their way to popularity—and this undoubtedly fuels the nagging for more stuff that so many parents experience. It also contributes to lots of heartbreak and confusion for many kids who equate "fitting in" with deeper and more durable friendships.

## I AM WHAT I OWN

The quest for friendship easily goes awry when kids make the mistake of believing that friends can be attracted through money or things. Kids are often fooled into thinking that if they have all the right clothes, makeup, CDs, or toys, they'll magically have the right friends. Middle school students struggling so mightily to establish their independent identities are especially vulnerable to this kind of thinking. And no wonder: As *Wise Up to Teens,* a book for corporate marketers, points out, about half of ads aimed at teens focus on friendships or romantic relationships, and just about all of them are about what makes someone cool. An inordinate amount of marketing to kids is focused precisely on this early adolescent age group as well, seeking to shape kids just as they are at their most tender developmental stage. When kids are subjected to thousands of ads each week, each telling them that they can buy their way to friendship and popularity, it's no wonder they nag and pester and push parents to buy them the right stuff. From their perspective, their whole social life is at stake!

Since we as parents know that our kids can't buy their way to real relationships, we need to help them find a more authentic path to fulfillment. We can start by teaching them the real nature of friendship. What is a true friend? In his book *You and Your Adolescent,* child psychologist Laurence Steinberg wrote, "A friend is someone who likes you for yourself, understands when other kids are making fun of you and giving you a hard time. A friend is not someone who judges you by what you wear or whether you go along with the crowd, tries to get you to do things that will hurt you or get you into trouble, or deserts you when the going gets tough."

Talk with your kids about friendship versus popularity. Use an example from your own childhood. Help them distinguish between "being cool" and being a true friend. Sometimes parents need to weigh in on friendships, monitoring the relationships to make sure nothing is amiss. If you suspect your child is making questionable compromises in order to fit in with a particular group, try to size up what risks might be associated with this behavior. If you suspect the use of drugs or other destructive behaviors, remember that you are the parent and exert your authority. You need to know where your kids are and with whom. Ask that they call in. Set a curfew. Talk to them about your concerns without talking at them. Remember that when dealing with this complicated situation, your goal is to get your children to talk. That means you need to listen. If you worry about your son's or daughter's friends, try to have a conversation that is probing, rather than controlling. You might ask, "Why do you think I don't want you to get together with that friend?" Sometimes you simply have to call a halt to relationships that are clearly destructive. The initial protest should give way to relief if your insights are correct and if you then offer your child freedom and opportunities in other ways.

Generally, our children are very adept at seeing and knowing the truth, just as Elizabeth (age fourteen) does: "I've heard people say that money can buy you friends; well, they're wrong. As soon as all your money is gone, guess who will be gone also, your friend. A real true friend will be there whether you have money or not. That's what's important, and that's what I want that money could never buy."

## BEST FRIENDS

Child psychologists say nothing is more important than having one or two good friends to see one through the storm of adolescence. Teenagers, especially, who have supportive friends or just one good friend are less likely to be influenced by the crowd. Nikki, fourteen, has found just such a friend: "What I really want that money cannot buy is a best friend. Very few people actually have a best friend. The few people that do do not realize how lucky they are. I have found my best friend. I know everything about her from when she was born, to where she wants to get married. She knows everything on me, and she can tell me anything. We don't go to the same school, so we get along much better. We know we will always have something to talk about. I usually have a better day knowing she will always be there for me to

Artist: Jacqueline, age 12

talk to. We have known each other for six years, but even all this does not make us better/best friends. It helps, but being absolute best friends means being able to tell them anything. . . . I love having someone there for me, a shoulder to cry on, and a pat on the back. I never feel lonely because I know she is there. The 'best friends' title should be taken seriously, remember that."

Parents have a role to play in helping kids find these special connections and in guiding them through the minefield of capricious cliques that dominate early adolescence. Help your children identify one or two loyal friends they know they can trust, that they share common ground with, who will be of help to them, and who they can count on over time. Talk to your kids about friendship, speaking about trust, reciprocity, communication, and other key ingredients in good relationships. Remind your child that the best way to find a friend is to be one!

## KIDS' PETS

Sometimes, when friends let us down, pets can serve as the next best thing. As you will see from the impassioned responses we got about dogs, relationships with pets are also very important in a lot of young lives. Animals can offer comfort, loyalty, and fun. Though not a substitute for human pals, pets can be true friends. Listen to what Jenna, a sixth grader, wrote about her pets: "What I want that money can't buy is a dog's love. A dog will always be there when you need it and is a good friend who could not and would not tell any of your secrets. I know from my own experience with my dogs that their love and loyalty mean everything to me and would to you too."

Rachel, fifteen, has a similar connection with her dog: "The thing I would want most is for my dog Misha to live through my whole life until I am at least ninety years old. I am only fifteen years old at this time, and my dog has made those years very special. When I am upset, she is there to comfort me. When I am happy, she is always willing to play. . . . I am going to try to make the rest of her life as meaningful and plentiful and as joyful as she has made mine."

Fourteen-year-old Erika touches on why animal companions can mean so much: "My dog, Casanova, loves me. Sometimes I yell at him, and sometimes I hug him. But no matter what I do, he always wags his tail and comes running up to me. He has unconditional love."

## THE ELEMENTS OF FRIENDSHIP

Parents should not worry too much or get overly involved in establishing their children's friendships. No doubt, it can be hard to stand back and watch when your child is struggling with relationships. It's helpful to know that this journey is part of a developmental process and that a few hard knocks along the way are normal. Whether or not your child has difficulty making and keeping friends, there are things you can do to help without trying to control the whole process. Here are a few ideas you may want to consider:

- Make the time for relationships to blossom. Friendship requires shared experiences and regular interaction, so set up play dates or a play group or regular outings to a playground when your children are younger, encourage them to invite friends over themselves as they get older, and include your children's friends in some family outings or activities. The best way to help your kids develop friendships is to make sure they spend time with others in places and activities they enjoy. Here's Rebekah, eleven, on the subject: "People say that money buys you everything. I know that is not true. Money can never buy you love or happiness. You cannot go into a store and pay a person to be your friend. I mean you could, but I'd rather meet them under a big apple tree."
- Make your child's friends welcome in your home. Let your child's friends know you like them. At the same time, leave the kids mostly to themselves and respect their privacy.
- Baking some after-school snacks or buying a group pizza now and then is well worth the investment.
- Expect the house to get a bit messed up when friends are visiting.
- Help your children practice good manners, thoughtfulness, and courtesy. A little kindness can go a long way in winning friends. A simple "thank you," "how are you doing?" or pat on the back can let others know you're thinking about them.
- Teach your children good sportsmanship. (And model it yourself, at their events as well as in your own endeavors!) We're all too aware of the decline in sportsmanship in adults and kids alike, so it was uplifting to see the exchange of jerseys—and handshakes—at the 2002 World Cup soccer matches.
- Nurture a sense of empathy and compassion in your children and help them imagine what another person might be feeling. Some children in our contest learned empathy the hard way. Marissa, thirteen, learned through an extremely painful personal experience: Her friend Jaime was killed in a car accident. She learned empathy in a most visceral way, not only

from grieving, but also from the friendship itself: ". . . my friend Jaime . . . was such a special person. Jaime would never think only of himself. He was caring and considerate, always listening to what I had to say first, then offering his opinion." Having him back again is what she wrote that she wants that money can't buy.

- Point out that being a friend means being there in tough times as well as just for fun. Help your children learn how to be supportive.

- Emphasize trust, truthfulness, and loyalty. The best way to teach this is to practice it with your own friends, talk about these values with your children, and praise them when they demonstrate them in their own relationships (including with you or a sibling, as well as friends). It's what Katherine, fifteen, is looking for: "What I really want that money can't buy is to know who to trust, and who not to trust. It would be very helpful to be able to recognize who is speaking the truth. It's hard in the world today to know who to share things with and who not to."

- Get to know the parents of your child's friends. Attending school-organized events is one good way to do this (and participate in planning them—especially if there aren't many going on). You may want to meet with other parents and kids for a group outing. Sometimes the connection can be more low key, but reaching out to these parents can strengthen the bonds of friendship among children and sometimes lead to new adult friendships along the way.

- Be a role model. Kids learn from what we do more than what we say. Take the time to nurture your own special friendships. Working parents understandably often have trouble maintaining close friendships, frequently because our lives seem so squeezed. It's important for our kids (and us) to carve out time to see friends, to make a phone call, send a letter, meet for coffee. Our friends help keep us grounded even in the rush of daily life.

## THE TREASURE OF FRIENDSHIP

Much has been written on the collapse of community, on the growing hyperindividualism in America, and on people's feelings of loneliness. The best antidote to these trends is friendship. There is no sadness like being without a friend and no treasure quite so wonderful as having a faithful, fun-loving person you can count on. To know that we are understood and wished well, to know that someone likes us despite our flaws, to spend time having fun with someone dear are wonderful feelings. Friendship is, as Emerson wrote, not a thing of "glass threads or frost-work, but the solidest thing we know." Just what children want—and need—in a world of change.

## FOR FURTHER READING

*Making Friends,* Fred Rogers and Jim Judkis. New York, Paperstar, 1996.
   (Mr. Rogers helps preschoolers launch their social life in his inimitable Mr. Rogers style.)
*How to Be a Friend: A Guide to Making Friends and Keeping Them,* Laurene Krasney Brown and Marc Tolon Brown. New York, Little Brown & Company, 1998.
   (A practical resource about the ins and outs of friendships for the four- to eight-year-old crowd, "peopled" by dinosaurs.)
*Cliques, Phonies, & Other Baloney,* Trevor Romain. Minneapolis, Free Spirit Publishing, 1998.
   (A great source that helps kids ages nine to twelve understand the dynamics of friendships in those troublesome middle school years.)
*Best Friends, Worst Enemies: Understanding the Social Lives of Children,* Michael Thompson and Catherine O'Neill Grace, with Lawrence J. Cohen. New York, Ballantine, 2001.
   (A valuable tool for parents who want to better understand the complex terrain of pre- and postadolescent friendships.)

# Chapter 6

---

# Nature

*A mud puddle to jump in.*—John, 4

*A warm sunny day.*—Samuel, 6

*Rain.*—Katie, 10

*To learn how to climb a tree.*—Robi, 7

*A beautiful earth.*—Cheryl, 15

*Natural beauty.*—Julia, 12

*Earth conservation.*—Frances, 11

*To see the great depths of the ocean.*—Allie, 10

*A clean park.*—Trey, 10

*People to stop littering.*—Rosy, 13

*A clean world.*—Jennifer, 8

*An unpolluted world.*—Erin, 13

*To save the oceans.*—Kirsten, 13

"A mud puddle to jump in. It's springtime in Alaska but everything is still frozen." Artist: John, age 4

*To have humans and animals live with each other . . . in harmony.*—Kyle, 10

*The animals to be safe.*—Emmy, 6

*Trees.*—Chrissie, age 7

*Clouds, [which] let people see a mysterious beauty by looking at the sky.*—Chelsea, 10

*The grass, the trees, the water, the rain forests, and the rain, the snow . . . and the horses, the birds, the wolfs, the snakes, the frogs, the rats, the mice, the sharks, the fish, the whales, and the seaweed.*—Jeff, 9

WHEN WE WALK in the woods or look up at the stars, something magical happens. Perhaps it's the recognition that we're connected to something much bigger than ourselves. All of us have experienced a sense of awe that often takes us by surprise. Nature can be a source of strength, solace, joy, inspiration, and healing. The ability to turn toward nature in good times and bad is one of the most important gifts we can give our children. And it's a gift no one can take away.

As Carolina, twelve, wrote: "Money cannot buy the beauty of the earth, nor can it replace its delicate balance. No amount of money on the earth can compensate for the loss of its frail living things. Just like a butterfly. Once it is mishandled, it is never as beautiful as it used to be and cannot fly. The most treasured things on earth are best left alone. Money will never be able to improve on the beauty nor protect its frailty once it is lost."

Love of nature is universal, and kids of all ages want more access to the earth's beauty and mystery. Anastasia, age ten, captured this sentiment perfectly: "I want to play in the snow every winter. I want to swim in the ocean every summer. I want to plant trees in the park with my friends every spring. I want to jump in puddles every autumn."

Reconnecting with nature does not require a major outing to a national park or an overseas trip to see a rain forest. Nature can be found in the small miracle of a seed sprouting in a paper cup on your windowsill, or the ants crawling across the sidewalk. Kids can rediscover nature simply by getting away from electronic toys and going outdoors, rain or shine, into the fresh air.

Nature helps children experience feelings of adventure and

"UNITY." Artist: Graham, age 14

peace. Eric, age nine, captured the former: "What I want that money can't buy is a jungle bigger than the Amazon Forest. It would have Siberian tigers, leopards, lions, monkeys, penguins, etc. Every animal in the world would be in my jungle. The biggest and longest river would be in my jungle. In the river would be the biggest blue whale to the smallest guppy. . . . My jungle would have four parts. The first part would be like the Amazon jungle. The trees would have lots of vines and be taller than Sequoia trees. The second part would be like the Great Plains. The grass would be five feet tall. The third part would be like Yosemite. It would have tall trees and have a big water-fall; plus it would be the source of the river. The fourth part would be just like Antarctica. It would be freezing cold."

Annie, fourteen, evoked a more serene vision: "I want time to stand up on a green hillside and shout out to the world, to sit and watch the billowing white clouds fly past on a warm wind, or time to lie in the grass and watch ladybugs crawl up the strong green stalks."

Eight-year-old Nancy is on a similar wavelength: "What I really want that money can't buy is the stars. I love the stars when they shine bright in the sky at night. It is so beautiful to wish upon a star. It's like a diary except that you can't write in it like a book, but you can talk to the sky and share your feelings and thoughts. It's just a wonderful thing to have such beautiful stars."

Like these kids, children of all ages yearn for more time in nature, and for a healthy environment. Over and over kids wrote expressing gratitude for trees, rivers, and animals. They told about dreams of floating on clouds and swimming with octopi. Kids wrote of small but meaningful moments: smelling the breeze, watching the sunset, and playing in the park. We heard pleas for stopping pollution, waste, and uncontrolled development. Many kids described their own special places.

Eleven-year-old Emily captured her own special place in this essay:
It's a place you want to be. . . . Free in the backyard of 75 Town Line Road. . . . There, there is an acre of wildflowers! A patch of Christmas trees, used for Christmas every year. Then comes the soft, clean, cut grass. There is a half acre of wild blackberries and raspberries. The sugar maple trees could produce maple syrup, and were great to climb on. There were four willow trees, which were outstanding for taking a very relaxing nap. This is something money won't, can't, and never could buy. I used to live on 75 Town Line Road, and the memory I have is priceless.

This young girl already has a deep and lasting connection to nature. And she didn't have to venture any farther than her own backyard.

A child's feel for nature can get dulled in the midst of urban sprawl outside and plastic toys inside. In a poll of parents conducted by my organization, almost half admitted that their kids would prefer to go to a shopping mall rather than go hiking in the woods for a family outing. Some 80 percent of American households are now in urban or suburban settings, and many children spend their days under artificial light in school, only to come home and sit in front of electronic screens for the rest of the day.

This is particularly troubling with regard to child development, for a growing school of experts suggests that interaction with the physical substance of the living earth (e.g., rocks, trees, wind) is critical to the child's developing brain, intelligence, and imagination. In some sense the universe is still unfolding, and we are all part of it. Children and adults need to be connected to this living world. In *The Shelter of Each Other,* Mary Pipher, noted child development expert and psychologist (and kind contributor to this book—see the introduction), worries about children who are separated from nature: "Children cannot love what they do not know. They cannot miss what they have never experienced. Families need wild places to visit and programs that connect children to the natural world." It is our job as parents to urge our children back outdoors, into nature.

Nature is abundant. The natural world is within our grasp much of the time. It's just that we're often unaware. We have to slow down, heighten our senses, and pay attention. Kids are actually better at this than adults. Children naturally meander, follow their curiosity, and take a deep interest in things. Nine-year-old Rachel shared her enjoyment of the outdoors: "[What I really want that money can't buy is] the whole nature outdoors and this is why. It is pretty and I can have fresh air and make new friends, like birds, and deer, and squirrels as well. . . . I can look at the evergreens. . . . I can roll down a hill and splash into the water. . . . I can watch the trees wave back and forth and then I can play in a field of roses and blossoms. . . . I can climb trees. . . . I can draw on dirt and collect rocks, and if it snows, I can play in it. . . . When it is fall I can look at the pretty leaves. . . . I hope you think about nature as much as I do!"

This pleasure in exploring and savoring the small wonders all around us is often lost as we grow older, and we start to lose the sense of appreciation for the simple things in life. We rush by the very things that could touch us deeply if only we gave them half a chance. Sadly, it's getting drilled out of our children at an ever earlier age as they mature sooner and grow up with synthetic sounds, images, and experiences. For the sake of our kids—and for ourselves—we need to try to hold on to the wonders of nature. It's a beautiful thing when we do, as you can read (and see) from Brittany, sixteen: "What I want that money can't buy is the sea shore . . . the warm sand . . . piles of dried seaweed . . . calls of the sea gulls . . . white-tipped surf . . . the playful banter of sea otters . . . cool sea breeze . . . fresh, salty sea

"What I really want that $ can't buy is...the ocean." Artist: Lauren C., age 12

air . . . cold ocean water . . . sand dollars and colorful shells . . . the tide pool . . . the tall, bright green sea grass . . . sea anemones . . . and the echoes of barking seals."

If your children are young, all you may need to do is honor, respect, and encourage their innate sense of connection to the natural world. Crouch down with them to examine that worm on a rainy morning; stop to look—really look—at your neighbor's flowers; go to the park regularly; take walks in the woods; plant a pumpkin seed; collect rocks or shells; make a mud pie. Help them retain this link as they get older. If kids are not exposed to nature often, they may not even know that they want or need a connection to the environment.

Ecologists, environmental psychologists, and others suggest that we all have a natural attraction to and affinity for the natural world. Some studies suggest that if this built-in love of nature is not encouraged in the early years, the opposite, biophobia, may set in. In *Earth in Mind,* teacher and environmentalist David Orr explained, "biophobia ranges from discomfort in 'natural' places to active scorn for whatever is not manmade, managed, or air-conditioned." It is a tendency to "regard nature 'objectively' as nothing more than 'resources' to be used." Data from the Brookside Zoo in Chicago suggest that in extreme cases children's primary emotional reactions to nature are fear and aversion.

Keeping our kids connected to the natural world takes conscious effort. The average American child grows up in a home with two TVs, three tape players, three radios, two VCRs, two CD players, one video game player, and one computer (Kaiser Family Foundation, 1999). The average time spent in front of electronic screens (television, computer, video games) is nearly four and a half hours per day among two- through seventeen-year-olds, according to the National Institute on Media and the Family. Our new electronic world detaches children from natural sensory experiences.

As parents we must take steps to reconnect our kids to natural rhythms. We need to provide frequent access to gardens and parks, encourage "natural play" activities, and foster direct interaction with the environment, rather than merely teaching kids facts about nature.

There are an endless number of things to do and discover. Remember, your child doesn't need three weeks at wilderness camp to be in nature.

The following list gives you a few ideas to consider in getting started. Some may seem obvious, but the truth is we tend to overlook even the most basic natural connections. So choose the ones that appeal to your children and you and use them as a springboard to other activities.

- Picnic in a park. Take a weekend family hike or bike ride. Stay close to home or visit nearby watersheds, wildlife refuges, or trails.
- Focus on the seasons—the rhythms of the day and the year. Notice the changes in shadows cast by the changing orbit of the earth. Celebrate the equinox and solstice—the arrival or departure of light. (Check for community events.) Watch a sunset or sunrise.
- Go stargazing. Stay up late and just ponder the stars from a good dark spot, or look for the constellations, or plan ahead to witness the next unusual celestial event, such as a meteor shower.
- Bring nature into your home: care for an animal; collect rocks, shells, or fossils; or make a terrarium.
- Hang a bird feeder. We tend to take these creatures for granted—too often we barely even notice the regulars in our neighborhood. Children love getting an up-close look.
- Grow something: a kitchen herb garden, a window box of flowers, a backyard patch, a community garden—or just a bean plant in a paper cup. Let your child water the plants or help with mulching. Offer your child firsthand experience of soil, water, light, and the cycles of life—not to mention earthworms!
- Build a snowman.
- Experience the elements (earth, air, fire, water). Go out into the weather, dig in the dirt, watch the clouds, fly a kite, make a campfire, splash in puddles, and walk in the rain.

"Money Can't Buy Rain." Artist: Katie, age 10

- Get to know your particular part of the planet. Explore your local area and bond to special places by returning there again and again and viewing them from more than one perspective. Check out the geography of your own yard or block—what plants and animals are native to the area, for instance? Consider creating a wildlife habitat of native plants to attract birds, insects, small mammals, frogs, and turtles that belong on your little section of the earth.
- Grow and arrange flowers.
- Look, really look, at the world around you, the ground cover in your yard, the bugs in your grass, the trees across the street, the blue sky and moving clouds. Slow down. Listen. Smell. Hear. See.

# TEACH YOUR CHILDREN TO PROTECT THE ENVIRONMENT

Nickelodeon Television conducted a poll in 2001 that showed that concern for the environment is the number one issue for school-age kids ages eight to ten. And 90 percent of eight- to twelve-year-olds in another Nickelodeon poll believe that kids can make a difference in protecting the environment. Older kids rank other issues higher but consistently express ecological concerns. As parents, we should nurture this environmental impulse—both because our kids should help take responsibility for the earth and because their future depends on it. Start by helping your children to develop a deep personal appreciation for the natural world. The desire to protect it follows almost automatically.

Bradley, seventeen, painted a very clear picture of just what an environmentally responsible world would look like: "I believe that if every person in the world could somehow be instilled with real, genuine love and respect for nature, many of the problems facing our planet would be solved. . . . Here are some of the results that would follow: Consumers would buy only environmentally friendly products and only ones they needed. They would recycle more things more often, reducing the need for raw materials and landfill space. Elected officials would make decisions that benefited people and nature instead of big business. People in developed countries would get outside more often and reduce stress by getting in touch with nature. Hemp would be legal in the U.S. and could eventually replace forests as a pulp source for paper products. In other countries, people would stop destructive farming, logging, and hunting and work with the land instead of against it. Environmentally friendly farming techniques would preserve the land and produce a more stable food supply. Families would limit their size so that there would be more food and opportunities available to each person. These are just some of the things that could happen if the human race could reconnect with the earth and learn to love it again."

There are many ways to help children conserve resources and

care for the earth. Talk to your kids about the obvious: recycling, picking up litter, conserving water. Encourage them to be part of your household conservation efforts, from installing energy-efficient light-bulbs to limiting the use of pesticides and fertilizer on your lawn. Participate in neighborhood cleanups and beautification efforts and involve kids in gardening, including the planting of native plants.

What and how much we buy has a huge environmental impact. Kids need to be wise consumers, not just to protect their financial security but also to ensure their environmental future. Part of what they need to be taught is that some products are better than others, when it comes to the environment. For example, when you and your kids buy locally produced organic food from farmers markets, you are helping protect local farms and improve family health. When you and your children purchase recycled paper for your home computer, you're helping save forests. When you and your family drive an energy-efficient vehicle, you are helping prevent global warming.

Of course, *how much* we buy also has an impact, and this can be harder to get across. In a nationwide public opinion survey by my organization, two thirds of parents said their children care about keeping the earth clean—but 70 percent said their kids don't think that buying too much stuff hurts the environment. Kids should know that while Americans make up less than 5 percent of the world's population, we consume fully 30 percent of the earth's resources. If every person in the world consumed as much as the typical American, we'd need four more earths just to provide the resources—and absorb the waste.

When your kids are insisting that they must buy something, it's helpful from time to time to employ an environmental critique. Kids have a very strong sense of fairness and justice (we're all familiar with the plaintive cry of "That's not fair!"), so pointing out the inequalities in our current system should get their attention. Americans, for example, produce twice as much garbage as the average European and one fourth of the world's global warming gases. We are using more than our share of what the earth has—and that's not fair!

Sandra, a mother of a ten-year-old and a member of the Center for a New American Dream, told me that talking about these environmental connections has helped her curb her daughter's desire to shop for more clothes. "It's one more argument I can use when she's nagging me to buy her something she just doesn't need!"

## Responsible People in This World

What I really want that money cannot buy are responsible people in this world. People who will not litter. People who show love to this world. Things like potato chip bags, papers, etc., are things that need to be picked up. Not just one person should do that, but many others. . . .

I live in a house that . . . we rent. The house is owned by a foot doctor. . . . Well, we have a parking lot for my car to park, because we live there and spaces for the nurses, himself, and patients. I see people drop their garbage in the lot. It is very embarrassing not just for my family but for the owner of the house. It makes me upset to see garbage in the parking lot. I try to pick it up and throw it away, but the next day it has more garbage in it. It is useless. That is why I want responsible people in this world.

—Carolann, 10

I hope that people can change their attitudes toward the environment and nature. . . . I enjoy visiting my grandparents in Florida. I go kayaking in the canals around Lido Key in Sarasota. We play tag with the manatees, go crabbing, and explore sandbars. Unfortunately, we are not seeing as many manatees, the crabs are becoming scarcer, and the sandbars do not have as much marine life as they previously did.

The population of the area has grown. People are developing the waterfront properties and are ripping out the sea grapes and mangroves in order to build sea walls to protect their houses. The marine life needs these plants to live and breed. More people want bigger and faster boats for recreation. Unfortunately, the need for speed . . . has killed or injured a large percent of the manatee popula-

Money can't buy a Clean Park

"Money can't buy a clean park." Artist: Trey, age 10

tion. The boats either hit them or cut them with their propellers. The commercial fishing, to feed all these people, has all but wiped out the fish and crabs in these waterways between the islands and the bay. The commercial boats come into the canals with nets that stretch from one side to the other and strip the fish from the area. The crabs are dying because they no longer have the fish for their nourishment.

My dad and I have a fun time kayaking and exploring. We don't need to go 50 mph or have a huge boat to have fun. We enjoy the peace and beauty of nature.

There is no amount of money that will change people's attitudes toward this simplicity of life. The government cannot enact laws and force people to do the right thing. We must talk to our friends and have them talk to their friend, and in this manner, we can help change people's attitudes toward the environment. I hope I will always be able to enjoy kayaking in this area, but if people don't change, I don't see how I will be able to.

—Jamie, 11

Once your kids have heard about the negative, give them a chance to *do* something positive. Get them involved with like-minded kids through environmental clubs or organizations. Encourage them to connect their own actions and behavior to the health of the planet. Let them know that small actions by a lot of people add up to big change.

---

### My Big Question Is Whether Anyone Else Notices

As I stare from my backyard, I watch the once quiet suburban road being turned into a six-lane highway. The street, which used to be lined with trees from one end of the community to the other, will soon look like any other highway. The huge wetland area, which once dominated the east entrance to my town, is being converted into a mall. Am I excited? No, I'm scared. . . . How far are we from lowering the oxygen levels? What about the swamps we've dried up in order to build more developments? Almost every summer we have a drought, and then the forests catch on fire. The ocean that lies to the east of us was once beautiful but is now lined by dirty beaches and sea-lice-infected waters from the sewage. Dead sea life keeps surfacing on the sands, and dead animal life dots the highways. My big question is whether anyone else notices. . . .

I want absolutely everyone to realize that we have to protect the environment in order to have a future. I want my neighbors, friends, tradespeople, professional people, and government officials to STOP ignoring the problem. Instead, we must reeducate ourselves to save our world. We need to work together, and we need to care—and that doesn't cost anything!

—Samara, 15

---

Helping our children learn about and experience the natural world is one of the most important tasks we can take on as parents. And time in nature can be soothing for parents who are trying to do too much. So call some friends and hit the bike path, seek out a hik-

"A Warm Sunny Day." Artist: Sam, age 6

ing trail, or just linger at your window to watch a spider's web. There's magic everywhere, if we just slow down to enjoy it.

## FOR FURTHER READING

*How Much Is Enough?,* Alan Durning. New York, W.W. Norton, 1992.
(Perhaps the best book available describing the environmental consequences of a high-consumption society. This book is highly recommended for the adult reader.)
*Ranger Rick Magazine,* National Wildlife Federation, 11100 Wildlife Center Drive, Reston, VA 20190, www.nwf.org/wildalive
(A monthly nature magazine for kids ages seven to fourteen.)
*Ecology Crafts for Kids, 50 Great Ways to Make Friends with Planet Earth,* Bobbe Needham. New York, Sterling Publishing Co., 1998.
(Lots of low-cost or free craft ideas for connecting enjoyably with nature.)

## ADDITIONAL RESOURCES

The Center for a New American Dream, 6930 Carroll Avenue, Suite 900, Takoma Park, MD 20912, 1-877-68-DREAM, www.newdream.org

(The Center for a New American Dream has an online consumer action program for kids and adults and offers numerous educational materials and a video.)

www.kidsface.org

(Kids for a Cleaner Environment offers an excellent web site with hopeful environmental news from around the world.)

www.nwf.org/kids

(The National Wildlife Federation kids' page includes games and environmental news for children.)

www.ucsusa.org

(The Union of Concerned Scientists has an excellent Great Green Web game examining the environmental impact of consumer choices.)

Roots & Shoots, P.O. Box 14890, Silver Spring, MD 20910, www.vax.wcsu.edu/cyberchimp/roots/roots/html

(The Jane Goodall Institute's program for young people around the world.)

Earth Force, 1908 Mount Vernon Avenue, 2nd Floor, Alexandria, VA 22301, 1-800-23 FORCE, www.earthforce.org

(A national youth environmental advocacy organization.)

# Chapter 7

—————

# Spirituality

*I want peace, a quietness for my soul. An ease for my thoughts
and a rest for my heart. . . . I want faith. To possess the substance
of things hoped for and the evidence of things not seen.*
—Elisa, 14

WE LIVE IN A FRACTURED WORLD, and all of us need some moorings
in the journey through life. Most of us, including children, encounter
feelings of fear, pain, unworthiness, longing, and isolation somewhere
along the way. Kids want to share our search for inner peace and
meaning in the midst of life's inevitable ups and downs.

Judging from the many contest essays we received on this subject, children are yearning to understand how they relate to the larger
universe. Kids wrote about God, heaven, and the desire to be connected to some greater purpose. Some described feelings of gratitude,
while others sought forgiveness and healing. Some just wanted their
big cosmic questions answered.

Children need the time and space to nurture their inner lives.
This chapter will try to help you build such a place with your children, so that together you can examine life's deeper questions, experience new connections, and share your spiritual journeys.

Of the generation born after World War II, 95 percent received a religious upbringing, yet some two thirds of the seventy-five million American baby boomers left the religion of their parents by their early adult years, according to Dr. Wade Clark Roof, author of *Spiritual Marketplace: Baby Boomers and the Remaking of American Religion*. While many returned to the fold later, millions of baby boomers and younger American adults are experimenting with Eastern religions and independent spiritual practices. According to a report by the U.S. Information Agency in 1997, the traditional American three-faith formula (Catholics, Protestants, and Jews) is now obsolete. The number of Islamic mosques in the United States has doubled in fifteen years, and Buddhism and Hinduism are rapidly growing.

Faith and spirituality are deeply personal matters, and parents are clearly taking diverse approaches to helping kids explore their inner lives. Regardless of your own questions or doubts, you have probably sought serenity, understanding, and some sort of peace in the rush of modern life. Your children have the same spiritual needs.

## Joy and Wonder

I think I, and perhaps most other people, have lost [something] at some point in our lives that money cannot recover: a simple joy, amazement at the world around them. A sense of wonder. I remember recently watching a magician do his show in the park. As he made his audience gasp with fancy finger work, a toddler was crawling about in that toddler fashion searching out twigs amidst the grass. At each find she would stop, fascinated, examine, and carefully place the treasure in the pocket of her overalls before moving on to seek out more. This is wonder. We can't pay for it, because it is something intangible, priceless, a phenomenon we have lost. It is this simple joy that I plan to search out, and I know money cannot buy it for me.

—Kathryn, 16

Over and over the boys and girls entering our contest expressed a desire for inner peace and calm—however it comes to them. John, age fourteen, described it this way: "What I really want for not just myself but for all of the world is for us to all find inner peace in our hearts and to discover that we are not the Generation X but we will become the revolutionary generation who will be remembered through history, years from now, as the generation who pulled the world out from the deep abyss. . . ."

Kids want a source to lean on, give them hope, and make them feel safe. For many of them, like seventeen-year-old Danielle, this means a relationship with God: "In my life I have had many objects, but none of them can compare to the love and strength that I receive from our Almighty God. . . . My salvation is God. He fills all the holes and emptiness in my life. He is someone I can look to for comfort and happiness. God forms a sense of peace in my life. No amount of money can ever buy the love of God. . . . I have meaning to my life that I never would have thought possible."

Samantha, seven, was more direct still: "Money can't buy God because he is invisible, he is big, he is nice, he is strong, and helpful. . . ."

Others want greater happiness, security, and an assurance of heaven:

### Heaven

I want to be in Heaven with my God more than anything in the world. I would rather spend one day in Heaven than one thousand elsewhere. . . . In Heaven you would never cry again; you would never get hurt again; you would never be hurt again; you would never be lied to again. You would never be betrayed, never ever left alone. You would never bleed; you would never be scared, never think you can't go on. It is perfect and is totally separated from sin.

—Brian, age 14

"Money Can't Buy ME." Artist: Destiny

Today in life it seems like there is nothing money can't buy. But there are some things. There are some things like love. . . . beside that there is peace. . . . Then there is pride, honor, and respect, which is something you have to earn not buy. But there's one thing I really want [that] money can't come close to buying. Something I think about every day and when I have the precious Lord's name. Money can't buy my way into heaven. And that's something I really want.

—Destiny, age 12

## DEVELOPING AN INNER LIFE

Contemporary culture focuses on external appearances; an inward journey helps us stay connected to what really matters in our daily scramble. The inner life requires slowing down rather than doing more and is nurtured by an attitude of surrender rather than control. Children (and adults) need time and space in their lives to step back from the relentless cycle of trying to do, buy, and achieve more. Consider creating a quiet space in your home conducive to prayer, meditation, or simply the appreciation of beauty, and establish quiet times when the television and stereo are off and natural sounds of birds, wind, and rain can be heard. Encourage your children to be present in the moment, noticing the small wonders of everyday life.

Here's what Christina (age fifteen) had to say: "I wish people could just look around themselves and try to find true happiness within the little things in life. You will be amazed at what such simple things can do to turn that frown into a smile. You don't need money to make you happy. . . . True happiness comes from within. Not only can your family and friends make you happy, but you have to find that happiness inside first."

Nikki, sixteen, described what the world would feel like if we had more inner and outer peace:

*What would it be like, if it 'twas true?*
*The doves would dive through the clouds way up high*
*In front of the sun casting its golden hue*
*As it rises into the sky.*

*The wind would whisper*
*"Peace" it would say*
*As the grass wisps and stirs,*
*And the creatures look happily towards another new day.*

*Serenity would flow off of the people like rain*
*And around us the evil things*

*Like hurt, sorrow, loathing, and pain,*
*Would be replaced by warmth, love, kindness;*
*the emotions peace brings.*

## I'LL BE WATCHING YOU

As with so many other things, our own spiritual path is key to our children's. In this sphere especially, kids look to our stated values and beliefs as well as our actions and behavior as guides for their own spiritual growth.

We often complain about our children's hyperactivity and intense schedules, but what example are we setting? Are we slowing down enough to ponder life's deeper possibilities? When your child starts asking questions or getting interested in meditation or religion, consider it an invitation to reconnect to your deepest values and beliefs.

Our homes should be reflections of our values. Some practices are really universal. Offer help to others in need. Be an example of loving-kindness with your spouse, and when that's impossible (which happens to the best of us), try to find peaceful ways to handle house-hold conflict. Express gratitude openly. Notice and celebrate beauty. Do something to promote social justice and world peace. Offer hospitality to someone who differs from you—in age, race, or socioeconomic status. Be honest and kind as much as possible, and expect the same of your children. Try to live by the Golden Rule.

You won't always pull it off, of course, any more than my family does. We're all only human. But even—or especially—in times of exhaustion, anger, disappointment, or pain, try as much as possible to model your values and faith. When things go wrong, talk about the problems rather than avoid them. Your efforts—both failures and recoveries—are the core spiritual curriculum for your kids.

The spiritual journey is a very personal one. For most of us, it is a bumpy road to figuring out what is true, what is real, why we are here. Embrace the pleasure of journeying together and teach your children the truth about life as it unfolds for you, including the questions that sometimes seem to have no answers.

## LIVE THE QUESTIONS

Most parents have to cope with cosmic questions from their children. Is there a God? What happens when you die? Is there a heaven? If there is a God, why do so many people suffer? Many of us feel ill-equipped to answer these questions when we ourselves may be uncertain of the answers. But questioning is a key component of a spiritual life. Our role as loving parents is to honor the questions, nurture the lifelong search for—and experience of—truth and wisdom, and create the conditions for a positive spiritual life.

Most kids are naturally adept at questioning, especially when they are very young. Even if you feel you are not always providing the details they are looking for, all you need to do is try to answer their questions honestly from your own perspective. Help your kids not to shy away from the questions, but rather to embrace them. Don't underestimate what your kids can deal with in terms of uncertainty. They'll be able to hear you if you explain that some people think this, some people think that, here's what I think. . . . Talk to them also about your own understanding of faith, the nonanalytic and mysterious part of life, and the possibility of experiencing a sense of God or the sacred without having to understand all the details.

Your reward will be seeing them develop analyses of their own, the way Josh, fourteen, does: "What I want that money can't buy would be wisdom. When Solomon was offered the same thing by God over anything else in the world (like riches and wealth to hot chicks and a brand new Firebird), he picked wisdom. Wisdom is not something you can go down to the corner grocery store and buy. It is something that has to be learned through mistakes and accomplishments. It is something that is acquired over time. Wisdom is the understanding of what is true, righteous, lasting. Wisdom is just plain out common sense and good judgment."

## RITUAL

For most of us, weekends are spent rushing to get laundry, grocery shopping, and homework done in time for the start of yet another week. Weekdays are consistently a scramble to stay in high gear until Friday. Our crazy lives leave little time for practices or rituals that can provide structure and support for spiritual development. If you carve out a little time to establish a few rituals, you may find that they become anchors for your children now and in years to come.

The most obvious weekly spiritual ritual is going to some kind of service regularly. This assures time set aside for worship and reflection with a community of like-minded people, and time devoted to instilling values and beliefs that are important to you. Setting aside a weekly time for expressing thanks and seeking guidance is an important part of the spiritual journey.

In addition to weekly time-outs for worship with others, there are many simple, familiar practices that can help root adults and children alike.

- Give thanks by saying grace or pausing for silence at meals and before bedtime. There are several books of prayers and graces that can be shared with children.
- Consider reclaiming a Sabbath. Stop rushing around, put aside distractions, minimize obligations, and keep errands and chores to a minimum in favor of a day for rest, reflection, and renewal. As Rabbi Michael Lerner wrote in *Spirit Matters,* "For one day out of the week, don't try to change, shape, or transform the world. Respond to it with joy, celebration, awe, and wonder. Open yourself to the miracle and mystery of the universe." Real life may force us to handle a few things, but if you try to keep one day quieter, the mood will be different, and your children will have that precious time to meander, make music, or simply hang out and talk with you.
- Create commemorative spaces in your home, such as a wall of photos of ancestors, a family shrine, or a meditation space.

- Spend one time each week helping someone in need and involve your kids in the process. You may find that this weekly contact with someone who is suffering will deeply alter your sense of priorities and reorient you to what really matters in life.
- Create special spiritual ceremonies to commemorate births, passage to young adulthood, and seasonal events such as the equinox.

## FIVE SPIRITUAL PRACTICES FOR KIDS AND ADULTS

### Silence and Stillness

As the twenty-first century begins, the clamor of the Information Age and industry have combined to invade nearly every public space. Oddly, we seem compelled to let noise invade the inner sanctums of our homes as well. Yet silence and stillness are ancient paths to spiritual wisdom and understanding. There is absolutely no substitute for silence in the quest for insight and peace.

For me as a practicing Quaker, silence and stillness are central to my own spiritual tradition, and Buddhist and other Eastern traditions start from a similar place. No one needs any particular background or credentials to reap the benefits. And even the least-leisured, hardest-working person *can* do it—big blocks of time are *not* required. You can embrace silence and solitude by carving even tiny blocks of time out of your busy days. Five or ten quiet minutes in the early morning can make a surprisingly big difference.

Don't assume that meditative practices and quiet time are for adults only. This is an equal-opportunity activity for all ages (with the exception of the youngest children), and many families are working to help their children develop an appreciation of the process. My family attends Quaker meetings, and the long periods of silence are admittedly sometimes boring for my kids. Sometimes they goof off, become restless, and can't wait for the cinnamon buns served at the end of meeting! Sometimes, though, they seem to truly enjoy the process. And I believe that they are influenced by the family's commitment to a spiritual life, even when the process can be frustrating for them.

You can embrace silence in many ways; you don't necessarily have to be physically alone, sitting quietly, or closing your eyes. Establish some quiet zones during the week when televisions and CD players are off, phones aren't answered, and each family member is free to just be quiet. You'll be surprised to discover how soothing this can be.

Much has now been written about how "being" precedes "doing." It's hard to justify stopping when there's so much to do. It's challenging to surrender to the possibility of another dimension—one that may *only* be accessible through a stance of open, quiet humility. But try it, along with your kids, and feel yourselves awaken, your hearts soften, and for a few minutes, all thoughts and worries cast aside.

Plenty of books and tapes can tell you everything you might possibly want to know about meditation, if it interests you. Yet the basic premise is simple: sitting still, staying quiet, breathing in and out mindfully, bringing the mind gently back into the moment whenever it wanders—that's it. You're meditating. Breathe. Be present in the moment. Be receptive to whatever you are hearing, seeing, smelling, feeling, and let your mental turbulence just flow by and calm down. As Ram Dass, drawing on the Buddhist tradition, put it, "Be Here Now."

Older children pick up simple meditation techniques quickly and easily. I'll include a few here that I've used myself, and with my children, and you might find them useful too. One of my favorites that my children have responded to is to say to yourself, in time with your breathing, "Breathing in, I'm calming my body; breathing out, I'm smiling." (Thank you, Thich Nhat Hanh.) Continue by saying, "It is the present moment" as we inhale and "It is a beautiful moment" as we exhale.

Explain to your children that any time they are feeling stress, they can stop wherever they are and go through these phrases privately. No one even has to know. It calms them and helps them to know that in the rush of life, they can lean into silence, into the recognition that in the bigger picture, whatever is stressing them isn't so significant. It's a tool they can really hold on to and press into service as necessary.

## Singing and Music

If silence can be golden, so too can sound. I think many people discover something transcendent in singing, especially singing with others. It doesn't have to be overtly spiritual music to open the heart. If you haven't yet discovered the balm of singing, give it a try with your family. You may be surprised where it can take you. Your kids may think you're embarrassing or weird at first since singing is no longer a regular part of daily or school life, and since our children are more accustomed to the passive and electronic music that dominates our culture. But give it a try and see if they can experience exhilaration or connection through song.

If you're self-conscious about being a tone-deaf family (though personally, I don't think that should stand in your way when it comes to singing your heart out), you might try drums for a similar release. Rhythm is so universal, and we all know kids love to bang! And for some kids, it will qualify as "cooler" than singing.

You may also want to introduce your children to "quiet" music, such as classical or sacred music. Take them to concerts or performances. I have purchased a few CDs with quiet, meditative music. Both my children find these soothing and calming at the end of a busy day.

## Compassion

So much of our culture celebrates individualism and the ability to dominate others. Yet the spiritual life is rooted in love and compassion for others. How can we help our children to find a quiet harmony with other people, and to give a priority to living compassionate lives?

If showing compassion somehow registers as duty and grim responsibility, something is amiss. Acts of kindness often come from an inner notion of actually being lovable! Compassion for others comes naturally when we are connected to the sacred dimension of life and have found some peace with ourselves. The first step in helping our children to be instruments of love is to assure them that they themselves are beloved.

Of course, children are both selfish and selfless. They often focus on themselves until reminded to think of others. Yet they can show great generosity and consideration toward others, and when they put the needs of others first, they can experience pride, empathy, and self-worth. Caring for others helps children understand that at the core, all people are essentially the same and of equal value. To look away from those in need is in some way to look away from that deep and sacred connection. You'll find plenty of ideas on getting kids involved with helping others in the chapter on making the world a better place, so I won't go into details here. Just remember, as always, that it does not require monumental action to help your children grasp this core spiritual practice. Train your kids to recognize neediness—and then to do what they can to help. And let them know they are loved, that the universe is essentially a friendly place, and that when they share a smile or offer someone else kindness, they are part of something powerful at work in the world.

## Nature

Many people connect with the sacred dimension of life by spending time in nature. It evokes feelings of gratitude and gives us perspective on our small place in the larger scheme of things. Sadly, what was once taken for granted—open skies, trees, and fields and meadows—now must be sought out deliberately. If you are a family of urban dwellers, take the time to make sure you and your family are really connecting with the natural world. The chapter on nature gives details on how to do this, so here I'll just say that you should try to help your children notice how complex and extravagantly beautiful

"PEACE." Artist: Kathryn, age 9

the world is, and rediscover together the reverence, wonder, and transforming power of the natural world.

## Spiritual Education and Study

Humans have sought truth and universal answers for thousands of years. Those committed through faith to one religious tradition typically study and reflect on their religion's written wisdom—as found in the Bible, Torah, Koran, Bhagavad-Gita, Tao de Ching, and others. Yet even those who seek for themselves and their children a nontraditional spiritual path should still consider the study of written wisdom passed down through the centuries. Here are a few specific ideas for helping your children become rooted in a lifelong love of spiritual study and reflection:

- Read, study, and memorize. Memorization of poetry and Bible verses is something largely relegated to earlier generations, but there can be great value in holding fast to valuable verses. You might have your children make booklets of important passages that offer inspiration, comfort, or insight about life, whether from the New Testament, myths or fables, the Tao de Ching, a Thoreau essay, aphorisms, or a section of a speech by Gandhi. My children each have a hand-decorated booklet of various spiritual verses, including some of the old faithfuls such as the Twenty-Third Psalm ("The Lord is my shepherd . . .") and the Lord's Prayer ("Our Father, who art in heaven . . .") but also excerpts from other spiritual traditions and from social justice speeches, such as Martin Luther King's "I Have a Dream" speech. They have memorized most of them. My hope is that they will hold on to these words of wisdom and perhaps return to them in times of need or change. Consider doing a similar project with your children. Share some of your own favorite verses and discuss how they might be applied in daily life.

  You might be surprised at how insightful your children can be in interpreting what they read when it really strikes a chord with them. Consider what Allan, seventeen, wrote: "Faith, hope and love. . . . True faith is deep within a person. It holds on to a belief so strongly that indifference, persecution, or even death itself cannot release the grasp of the individual's assurance. Circumstance or temptation might cause a brief moment of doubt in an individual's faith, but this is superficial and temporary; the deep foundation of faith has not been moved. . . . True hope is tied to faith in its confidence that what is hoped for will be delivered. And the greatest of these is love. . . . True, real love digs beneath the surface of humanity. It is selfless, giving up one's self-interest for another's benefit. It is unconditional and absolute. 'All you need is love' is true if love is unconditional and selfless."

- Encourage your children to keep diaries of drawings or art that expresses their feelings about God, heaven, or the divine dimension of life. In our Quaker meeting, children were asked to make a collage to express their understanding of the Light, the Quakers' way of describing a higher power or the sacred. The children took right to the assignment and created inspiring and moving images.

- Keep a journal. Personal diaries of spiritual thoughts and feelings can be comforting to children and adults alike.

- Tell stories. For most of human history, parents told stories to children to entertain and teach them life's crucial lessons. Storytelling has been squeezed out in recent decades, yet stories help children make sense of the world. Try bringing this ancient tradition back into your home, at bedtimes, as part of holiday celebrations, or at a regular "story hour." Anyone raised with Bible stories knows the power of parables and stories. This is an easy practice to introduce at an early age. You can select books or stories that explore themes of love, human generosity, or faith. Make up your own stories. Seek out books that help your children embrace positive values, ideals, and faith.

One thing most spiritual traditions have in common is an emphasis on the nonmaterial. The spiritual journey is a search for meaning, connection, and love. If you want your children to let go of material obsessions, help them find another place to go.

Ultimately, the spiritual life—for kids and adults—is about surrender. It is not so much about giving perfect definition to a metaphysical reality, but rather it is about giving one's inner heart to the journey for meaning. It is about the mystery behind the surface of things that nobody has ever been able to fully fathom or define, though many have sensed, experienced, or developed a deep and abiding faith in that mystery. Some call it God, others call it a universal consciousness, while others simply call it love. Each person's cosmology is ultimately deeply personal. I have no wish to prescribe a particular path, but I feel it is important to point out that children are asking for some spiritual guidance. Many seem wide open, perhaps even more so than adults, to the possibility of something beyond the secular, something beyond the surface in life.

One of the great joys of a spiritual life is the ability, ultimately, to just let go of anxieties, cravings, fears, and doubts. Who among us doesn't yearn for this release? Our children want it too. Try suspending disbelief and relaxing into the "not knowing" while also trying to deeply embrace the divine, however you define it. You might sit with your children and simply say, "Let's open ourselves up to the possibility of love at work in the world. Maybe it's here, right now, in this space, if we just sit quietly and ask for it to come into our hearts. Maybe we have to slow down and be open before we can experience this dimension. Who knows? Let's try it." If this doesn't work for you, simply know that your child probably has an inner voice that's probing these questions.

Expose your children to the possibility of faith—the ability to believe in what we can't know—and the protection, trust, persistence, and hope that comes with it. Help them connect to something bigger than themselves. Prepare them to experience deep love, as both giver and receiver, and to know that they are deeply and permanently cherished. Help them find their own peace. There is a Buddhist blessing that I always find comforting: "May you be safe and protected. May you be peaceful and happy. May you be strong and healthy. May you take care of yourself happily while living on this Earth."

The last of the great Roman emperors—and famous Stoic—Marcus Aurelius (C.E. 121–180) wrote, "Honor the highest thing in the Universe; it is the power on which all things depend; it is the light by which all of life is guided. Honor the highest within yourself; for it, too, is the power on which all things depend, and the light by which all life is guided. Dig within. Within is the well-spring of Good; and it is always ready to bubble up, if you just dig." Help your children step back from the rush of school, electronic distractions, and materialism to pause and notice the many sources of Light, without and within.

I'll leave you with a verse and prayer by Daniel Martin, used here by permission of Mr. Martin. I think his verse captures part of our situation. Perhaps it will speak to you and your children too:

*We who have lost our sense and our senses—*
*Our touch, our smell, our vision of who we are;*
*We who frantically force and press all things, without rest for body or*
*spirit,*
*Hurting our Earth and injuring ourselves; We call a halt.*

*We want to rest.*
*We need to rest and allow the Earth to rest.*
*We need to reflect and to rediscover the mystery that lives in us,*
*That is the ground of every unique expression of life,*
*The source of the fascination that calls all things to communion.*

*We declare an Earth Holy Day, a space of quiet:*
*For simple being and letting be;*
*For recovering the great forgotten truths.*

## FOR FURTHER READING

*Prayer for a Child,* Rachel Field. New York, Little Simon Publishing Co., 1997, © 1944.
(A beautifully illustrated prayer just perfect for young children of nearly any religious tradition.)
*Guide My Feet: Prayers and Meditations on Loving and Working for Children,* Marion Wright Edelman. Boston, Beacon Press, 1995.
(A collection of prayers and meditations from the president and founder of the Children's Defense Fund.)
*Simpler Living, Compassionate Life: A Christian Perspective,* edited by Michael Schut. Denver, The Morehouse Group, 1999.
(An inspirational collection of short essays on nonmaterialistic living from a Christian perspective. This book includes a study guide for groups and individuals.)

*The American Paradox, Spiritual Hunger in an Age of Plenty,* David Myers. New Haven, Yale University Press, 2000.
(An in-depth review of materialism and radical individualism with recommendations for redirecting the nation's moral and social compass.)

*A Path with Heart: A Guide through the Perils and Promises of Spiritual Life,* Jack Kornfield. New York, A Bantam Book, 1993.
(An extremely helpful book on meditation, inner transformation, and the integration of spiritual practice with the American way of life.)

*Graces: Prayers and Poems for Everyday Meals and Special Occasions,* June Cotner. New York, HarperCollins, 1994.
(A delightful collection of short graces and benedictions, suitable for children.)

*Responsible Purchasing Guide for Faith Communities.* Takoma Park, MD, Center for a New American Dream, 2002.
(Outlines eight easy steps congregations can take to protect both people and the planet.)

## ADDITIONAL RESOURCES

Omega Institute, 150 Lake Drive, Rhinebeck, NY 12572-3252, 800-944-1001, www.eomega.org
(A retreat center offering workshops and programs on values, meditation, and spirituality. Predominantly for adults but some children and teen programs available.)

Kripalu Center for Yoga and Health, Box 793, Lenox, MA 01240, 800-741-7353, www.kripalu.org
(A retreat center specializing in yoga and Buddhist practices.)

# Chapter 8

## To Make the World a Better Place

*I want the world . . . filled with these things: Friendship . . . Happy families . . . More magic . . . Generosity . . . Freedom . . . Love . . . Joy . . . Peace . . . Understanding . . . Hope . . . Clean air . . . Animal rights . . . Trust . . . Honesty . . . Fairness.*
—Katie, 9

*We need to work together to make the world a better place.*
—Dawn, 11

*But most of all I want everybody to have a home and food and some clothes.*
—Samantha, 7

CHILDREN KNOW HOW to dream big. An amazing number of kids are ready to take on the world's problems, including poverty, war, and racism. All people—children as well as adults—want the world to be a better place. We dream of a world with more peace and less conflict, more justice and less hunger, and more cooperation among all people. Being connected and concerned for those in need helps children discover untapped empathy, compassion, and sometimes courage. And it almost always puts material goods in their proper perspective.

Consider what Xandy, eleven, wrote: "What do I want that money can't buy? There are so many things I could do for myself that would make life happier, but why? I don't need it. It's just something nice for me. It would also make me much happier if I did something for someone who needs it.

"I'm sure you've seen all those homeless families all over the world. I'm sure all those people have many dreams, and it would be awesome for at least one of each person's dreams to come true! I'm sure they probably feel hopeless and worthless right now, but if one of their dreams came true it would make them feel special and change their outlook on life. It would be great if they fulfilled their dreams and lived their lives knowing that they are special just like everyone else."

Kids definitely want a better world, but many wonder if it's really possible to get one. They yearn for positive changes, but many don't see how they can really make a difference. Adults often share these quiet doubts and feelings of hopelessness. Can we actually make the world better for our kids and their kids? Can any one family make a difference? Is it worth the effort? The answer to these heartfelt questions is yes! There are a number of ways you can support your kids in this direction. Start with whatever fits your child and your family, whether it is community service, charitable giving, political action, or simply nurturing a sense of connection. This chapter will help you and your children make a difference.

## WORLD PEACE

If you have any doubt that children are deeply concerned about world peace and global conflict, consider the events set in motion by September 11, 2001. According to a study by Sesame Workshop, which involved children drawing pictures in the weeks and months

"… No more shootings and killings, just peace." Artist: William, age 11½

after the crisis, young people were deeply traumatized by the airline hijackings and the collapsing buildings shown on TV dozens of times. The subsequent talk of nuclear war and the Iraq conflict also caused much distress, especially among older kids. If you're old enough to remember diving under school desks as kids during air-raid drills, as many of us did in the late 1950s, you will surely sympathize.

Kids may not talk overtly about it, but many of them are deeply aware that the world is not a peaceful place. Kyle Pruett, a child psychiatry professor at the Yale Child Study Center who consulted with Sesame Workshop on the research, is quoted on the Children's Health Fund web site as saying, "It's hard to say whether their feelings about September 11 will go away. They're like children raised on the San

Andreas fault. Every tremor they feel from now on may evoke fear."

Although the kids in our contest wrote their essays before September 11, 2001, an overwhelming number identified world peace as the number one thing they want that money can't buy. Over and over, entries addressed creating a peaceful world, with each child conceptualizing what that means in her or his own unique way. Kristen, twelve, wrote: "I don't mean just between countries. I mean peace in schools, companies, counties, etc." To Gianna, ten: "World peace means people would get along with each other. Everyone should be friends. I would hope we will never see wars in our community. . . . If we had world peace we would all live in harmony and our Earth would be an even better place to live." For Jimmy, eleven, the idea is more visceral: "If we had world peace then we wouldn't have to ever worry about being shot or bombed. It's sad to see people on TV without homes or food. I wish it would just end. People die each day during a war for no reason. . . . I really wish that not just I, but everyone can have this dream." For eleven-year-old Armend, it's personal: "I want Independence in my country (Kosovo). Independence is something that you can win and not buy. A lot of people died to win Independence for their country. . . . I don't want any more people to die."

Brenden, twelve, sums up children's desire for peace: "World peace . . . would allow children to grow up in a better world than it used to be. It would allow people to walk around their neighborhood at night. . . . This would put an end to wars, guns, and hatred that our little world is so filled up with. This would also bring countries that were enemies to one another closer together and give all countries the same human rights that we have in the United States of America. World peace sounds like a good idea to me."

## CRIME AND PERSONAL SAFETY

For a lot of kids, world peace begins with eliminating crime and violence in our own country, and creating peace and safety in all of our neighborhoods. As Shaun put it: "I want to know that I am safe. I want the security of knowing I can go to school, or to the mall (with my family), and come back safely. I just want to live in a safe world and not have to fear violence or crime."

Many kids pinpoint guns as the problem: "I wish nobody made guns," wrote Rashan, ten. Emily, twelve, seconds that motion: "What do I want that money can't buy? . . . being able to walk in my classroom in the morning, knowing that the kid just down the hall does not have a gun in his pocket, backpack, or anywhere. I want the schools of America to be safe. Not by security guards in every school, but by educating the kids of America. . . . I would like to be able to be confident that there will not be . . . another killing of another person's life because of who they are, or what they look like. I want the schools of America to be safe."

Even kids who feel secure in their own homes and schools and neighborhoods most of the time still have lingering fears, and compassion for those in less certain circumstances. Shannon, twelve, explained the duality as well as anyone: "If I could have one thing that money couldn't buy, it would be for the world to be a better place without any of the crime and violence that is going on. Some nights I go to sleep wondering if my friends and family will be alive to see tomorrow. I even wonder if I will, and that is coming from a person who lives in a very safe neighborhood with police officers as neighbors, but I still get scared. . . . I mean just last week a first grader in another school shot and killed a classmate because she had told him to get off her desk. . . . I just wish that somehow other people could have a life as good as mine and that people could understand that everyone has feelings and they can be hurt as easy as one, two, three or A, B, C. But, unfortunately, I am not as innocent as I may seem. I used to make fun and pick on people just like everybody else has before in their life. As I get older, I have been more understanding and have treated people the way I would like to be treated, but some people don't even seem to care. I hope that someday . . . [my] children . . . will . . . be judged for the person they are on the inside and not for the person they appear to be."

"NO MORE GUNS!!" Artist: Phillip, age 11

What I really want that money can't buy is a peaceful and contented world. Everyone would be friends; our neighbors would be like family. We could walk anywhere, anyplace, anytime, without feeling scared, unhappy, or unsafe. People would learn to cooperate, to overcome prejudice, and to love each other. Nobody would be either rich or poor. If someone were sick or disabled, the whole community would pitch in and give what they have to give. We would have no use for ghastly places like prisons or slums. The police and the FBI would do different things than they do today. Guns, drugs, and weapons would be banned. Nobody would think of using them. They would lie in the dust, forgotten. War and crimes would be abolished, something of the past. If only people learned to respect peace and people the way they are, on the positive side, the world would most certainly be a much better place.

—Sasha, 11

## RELIGIOUS AND RACIAL HARMONY

The next most common theme picked up by the kids writing about making the world a better place was "friendship between peoples of different colors, races, and religion" as Araceli, twelve, put it, or "unity" in fourteen-year-old Graham's words. Again, each entrant had a unique spin on just what this would look like:

Shannon, ten: "I want [everyone] to understand that we're all equal and just because someone has a different color of skin doesn't make them any different."

Makalyla, seven: "What I really want that money can't buy is for people all over the world to treat each other with love and respect."

Aimia, fourteen, made it personal: "What I really want that money can't buy is harmony, racial and religious harmony. . . . The skin that protects us comes in all different shades. It's the difference in the shades that makes the world so beautiful. Like roses in a flower shop. Red ones, yellow ones, pink ones, but they are [all] roses. . . . My sister is Japanese. My sister is Czech. My sister is Brazilian. My brother is Albanian. My brother is Macedonian. I am American. Our mother is Jamaican; we all call her Mom. We are Buddhists, Muslims, and Christians. We are one family. We live together and we learn from each other. What I really want that money can't buy is racial and religious harmony. Like in my house."

## COMMUNITY SERVICE

Volunteer service by young Americans is up 12 percent over the last ten years: 74 percent of college freshmen volunteered their last year of high school in 1998, versus 62 percent in 1989, according to UCLA/Higher Education Research Institute's Annual Freshmen Survey, although only 21 percent reported mandatory service work as a graduation requirement. Seventy percent of young people ages fifteen through twenty-one have participated in activities to help strengthen their communities at some point in their lives, according to 1998 figures from Do Something/Princeton Survey Research.

Involving your children in community service just requires tapping into their passions and talents and directing them toward tutoring, getting out the vote, reading at a day care center, volunteering at an animal shelter, or working at a soup kitchen. When kids find a good match, the experience can touch them greatly, as it did Jennifer, fourteen: "I have been volunteering at a nursing home for three years. I receive great satisfaction from being with these older people, and they make me feel really special. They don't ask for much out of life— just a little love, patience, and time. I spend my time just being there for them and doing what pleases them, such as brushing hair, walking, talking, or most of all listening to their accounts of their lifetime. Most of these people contributed greatly to society during their prime time. Now that they are old . . . some of them are forgotten. People are very busy with their day-to-day lives and don't have time to spend with them. I would like to see more compassion and kindness shown in the world, especially to the elderly. It won't cost anyone any money, and the rewards are great."

You don't have to wait until your children are a certain age before they can pitch in. Kids of any age can pick up litter or pull weeds. Older children can choose their own opportunities for service.

Consider volunteering as a family (giving the added benefit of family time together in addition to doing something meaningful). Check out your local volunteer association, social service agency, or environmental group. The possibilities are limitless.

## CHARITABLE GIVING

You can donate money as well as time as a family. Many Americans are doing just that: 89 percent of households report making charitable gifts, according to Independent Sector's web site. Charitable giving, both in total dollars and in percentage of income, is higher in the United States than in any other country in the world, except possibly Israel, according to Robert Wuthnow and the Generous Giving web site.

Make sure your kids know about the charitable giving you do, and involve them to the extent you can, depending on their age. For example, when my husband and I decided to donate, rather than spend, our six-hundred-dollar 2001 tax rebate, we had a family discussion about how to direct it. You might let each child pick a recipient for some portion of the money you give away in any given year. Even if you are on a tight budget, giving financially at a very modest level helps others in need and gives children a sense of belonging to a larger human family. Money can be used in many ways. Do what you can to teach your children the joy of giving it away.

Val, a seventh grader, wrote about sharing what we have with those who have less, taking a global view: "What I really want that money can't buy is to have everyone help one another. So many people won't help those in need. If everyone pitched in, the world would be a much better place. Lots of people are so involved in their own lives that they forget about other people who need help. Some people say, 'God helps those who help themselves.' I don't believe this. If there are no jobs for people in some places, how are they supposed to make money? It doesn't grow on trees! Helping someone could be as simple as giving money or lending a hand. It could be as complicated as going to another country to help people. I have heard at church that the world has enough resources to support the world. These are things like money, building materials, or even human talents. People less fortunate would be in much better shape if everyone were to chip in a little to give their own resources, economic or otherwise. The people would be able to build warm houses, buy good food, and get proper health care. I think the world would be a much better place if everyone were more compassionate!"

## BEING PART OF THE POLITICAL PROCESS

Most young Americans are generally not engaged politically, even though they often care about the issues. Only one in five eighteen-through twenty-four-year-olds voted in the 1998 elections, and estimates show that 28 percent voted in the 2000 elections, continuing the downward spiral in youth turnout evident since the 1960s. Recent studies show a steep decline in basic civic awareness and action. But parents can encourage civic participation. For younger kids this may mean just talking about whatever your involvement is, getting them to help mail a letter you've written to an elected official, bringing them on a march with you, or taking them with you when you vote. Older kids may want to volunteer on a political campaign, e-mail a representative, speak at a school board meeting, or join a rally. Follow up on your kids' interests and concerns—protecting the environment, for example, or working to limit advertising in public schools. Help them find their voice—and learn how to use it. As emerging citizens, kids need to learn about how our society works, and their rights and responsibilities within it.

As Bradley, seventeen, put it: "Many people today simply don't care if they think they can't make a difference. But if we could somehow communicate to them that the earth needs their help and they can make a difference, things would be a lot different in the world."

Gabriela, thirteen, agrees: "Money can buy a lot of things, but it can't buy the way that we humans act. If there is one thing that I want that money can't buy, it is for us to learn how to live and cooperate with the world to which we belong. For if we could learn those few simple things and follow them all through life, would the world not be a better place? I think so."

## EMPATHY

One underlying theme all families can focus on is developing deep empathy and cultivating compassion for those who are less privileged. It is in empathy and compassion that action takes root.

There's a balance to be struck—exposing your children to poverty, hunger, homelessness, and so on, while empowering them to do something about these problems. Empathy is natural to kids (it is we adults who sometimes have conditioned ourselves to overlook uncomfortable truths), but you may have to help your children when it comes to finding an appropriate action to go with their feelings. Kids like Sarah, fourteen, who wrote, "What I want that money can't buy . . . [is] the end of human suffering," most likely need some guidance in figuring out how to pursue that dream.

Sometimes it helps to make our outreach deeply personal, to help bring the issues alive for both us and our kids. Spend an evening at a soup kitchen, visit a nursing home, or just get to know someone who is struggling to make ends meet. It can be transformative for you and your children. It may change your answers to the questions How much is enough? and What do I really need? Giving to another person or working to change the system in positive ways taps into the better part of us.

Elizabeth, nine, learned these lessons in her own home. Like all kids, the most powerful messages she received came from what she saw her parents doing:

"My dream is that all orphans would find a family. I am one of eight children. There used to be only three children in the family [I was the youngest]. Then my mom and dad decided to adopt a child.

After a lot of paperwork, they went to Russia and came back with my new younger sister named Lydia [2]. Then my parents decided to adopt again. After about a year, my parents went to Russia again. They came back with four more Russian children, Alexay [9], Nicholas [7], Katya [6], and Andrew [5].

"If all orphans could find a family, they would have someone to love them, someone to spend time with, and someone to be with them when it is needed the most. They would also have somewhere to belong, be cared for, remember, go back to, and think of, and somewhere to get their education. When you are in an orphanage, you do not always get those things.

"In my dream I wish that people would want more children, and that they would realize that there is always more room in the heart for more children even if it does not feel like it. I wish people would realize that all children need love, and that some children haven't experienced any love. My parents helped a lot in adopting, and I wish that everybody would, in their heart, want to do the same."

Having an experiential—not just theoretical—connection is important. But while children are gathering personal experience with the less fortunate (which is especially key for kids in affluent areas leading relatively sheltered lives), you should also take every opportunity to talk about the world's problems and share your analysis of potential long-term solutions.

When kids see headlines about bioterrorism, war, or any number of grave problems, they need your help to process the material; completely on their own, they often lack sufficient knowledge of causes or potential solutions. Talk to them about the problems they see in their community and schools, or hear about in the media. As children get older, they understand and analyze more, and in more complicated ways. They begin to grasp the root causes, as well as the surface symptoms. But at every step of that development, they need to have the chance to bounce their ideas off others, ask questions when they need to, or seek reassurance.

Some parents fear the effect exposure to harsh realities will have on their kids and wonder if it's better to shelter them for as long as possible. This is a natural inclination and stems from our love and our heartfelt longing for a safer, simpler world. While it is important not to paralyze kids with too much negative information or let them immerse themselves in bad news, you also shouldn't try to cut them off from it altogether. For one thing, you can't. For another, it's a disservice to them. Perhaps you know the ancient story about Buddha: His father so completely concealed from him the darker side of life— not letting him know that all people get old, sick, and eventually die—that when he finally found out the truth, he was so horrified that he fell into a deep depression for quite some time.

We must help our children grasp the world's problems without overburdening them with too much bad news. This is yet another challenge for parents, especially when television news tends to dish up nonstop footage of disasters, wars, and human tragedies. Television newscasters have learned that images of doom, violence, and various scandals "sell," but the toll on America's children may be higher than we yet fathom. On a personal level, I remember resenting the sensational news coverage of the Monica Lewinsky affair and its impact on my children. Many of my friends went to great lengths to protect their children from the nonstop footage of the World Trade Center disaster.

Leon Botstein, the president of Bard College, observed, "No generation of young people has been subjected to as much adult discouragement as today's schoolchildren and college students. Hopelessness and skepticism are nearly invincible foes of young people trying to find their place in the world." The British novelist Graham Greene defined melancholy as the "logical belief in a hopeless future." That hopelessness may explain, in part, the fact that approximately 20 percent of our children require professional mental health services, according to researcher William Capps. It's critical to remember that young people are inspired when parents or teachers help them imagine new possibilities for the world and translate those visions into action. As parents, we must calibrate our kids' exposure to the ills of the world while involving kids and others in positive endeavors to solve problems.

## ONE STEP AT A TIME

Don't get stopped by the immensity of some of the problems we're facing. Positive change almost always comes about one step at a time. The first step, both for you and your children, is to dare to imagine a future that is unlimited, where change is possible and human beings can overcome problems by working together. As Margaret Mead said, "Never doubt that a small group of thoughtful committed citizens can change the world. Indeed, it's the only thing that ever has."

Try to create an atmosphere at home in which your children can hear messages of hope and possibility. Speak to their highest ideals and talk of honor, truth, service, and democracy. The hunger to make a difference exists in all of us. So it is important for all of us to have small things we can do in any number of arenas that really do matter. We all need the experience of doing something positive and knowing that it touches someone else's life. Too often it's easier to talk about taking action than to actually do it. Here are a few ideas for getting started:

- Tell your kids stories of positive change and how it happened. Read and talk about the great historic leaders, by all means, but also ordinary people and how change can start with someone entirely outside the system as well as atop it. (Think Gandhi, Nelson Mandela, Susan B. Anthony, Rosa Parks.) Give examples you've witnessed in your own life. Check out books on people who have changed the world by virtue of heroism—and small acts.

- Partner with other families. Isolation contributes to hopelessness. When we gather with others to clean up a playground, march for a cause, or call for changes in the local school system, we are tapping into the power of people working together. In my neighborhood, families have gathered every year during the holidays to make gift boxes for kids in a nearby homeless shelter. Our children are very involved with this project and look forward to doing their part. My son and daughter have also joined my husband and me at various marches, rallies, and public meetings. At the Million Mom March they made and carried placards, and we marched with other families. When they saw the U.S. Capitol grounds swarming with parents and kids calling for an end to gun violence and restrictions on handguns, they were moved. I could see it in their faces, as they read the personal testimonies of families who had lost someone to gun violence, and as they listened to inspirational speakers demanding change. Adults were standing up to say *no* to more Columbines, *no* to reckless gun policies, and the kids in the crowd felt safer and more optimistic as a consequence. Even when victory isn't immediate, kids and adults are uplifted by knowing we are part of something bigger than ourselves and that thousands of other people share our views and values. So team up with other families to help out. You can start a social service project, get involved with improving your community, or link up with a national nonprofit organization tackling a problem that your kids are especially concerned about. Our nation is blessed with scores of groups tackling social problems. Find one and get connected.

- Track the positive impact of what your kids do. Whenever possible, get the results of their efforts. How much money did the school raise, and what was it used for? How many families did the scout troop help feed with its food drive? Is there any data on the health of the stream your neighborhood pitches in to clean up several times a year? Did the homeless shelter go all year without having to turn away anyone, thanks to its roster of volunteers? My organization has an online environmental action program for kids (www.newdream.org) that tracks how much energy, water, and trees they save by changing household consumer behavior. Kids like the immediate feedback. Making the connection for your kids that they have done something significant and important will be invaluable.

## LET IT BEGIN WITH ME

Since September 11, 2001, the world has felt less stable. Conflicts between countries and ethnic groups have increased, and the global economy has been shaky. Children read the headlines and often watch television news. They know that things aren't right in the world. As parents, how do we respond to a climate of fear? I don't think anyone has the total solution, but every family can take steps to make a difference in the world. Since so many children wrote in about the need to stop violence, both in their communities and at the global level, I've offered a few suggestions for addressing this issue at the family and community level. What I'm really suggesting are ways that young people can think about the biggest, thorniest world issues. You can adapt the following ways of thinking to whatever world issue concerns your child, be it religious and racial harmony, world hunger, or housing for the poor. Encourage children in these ways:

- Help your children to understand the issue, in this case the root causes of violence and injustice. The UN and the World Bank report that the number one cause of violence internationally is poverty and human suffering—and that alleviating poverty is one of the most powerful ways to reduce war and terrorism. The same is probably true here at home. Teach your children about sharing our wealth with those who have less. Ultimately, this is a political discussion, for as parents, we must try to help our children grasp the distinction between two types of destruction: destruction rooted in the human psyche and destruction tied to institutionalized greed or injustice.

- Teach your children to think about the issue first in personal terms. What leads to peace in their own lives, at home, and at school? The same things tend to matter on the world stage as matter in an individual's life, things such as fairness and sharing of opportunities and resources. Help them see where peace is in practice in their everyday lives. Anastasia, ten, had one idea: "I want to adopt a homeless dog and a little kitten from a shelter (mom, please let me!) and teach them never to fight."

• Help your child practice the values and changes they want for the larger world. Help them with peaceful conflict resolution. Teach your child how to settle problems productively, and without resorting to violence. Urge your child to reach out to other children who have problems, need friends, or are isolated in some way. Encourage them to make eye contact, smile, say hi, especially to the "unpopular" kids. These basic kindnesses and human connections are acts of peace. One person's kindness moves others to be kind. Reaching out to those less popular, just acknowledging their presence, is a basic act of peace in a world where alienation can have tragic consequences. Help your children to examine their own lives and take stock of the ways they help sustain peace and avoid violence: soothing someone who is upset, working out problems peacefully, or reaching out to those in need.

• Take some form of public action. Have your child write a letter to your elected official about his or her urgent desire for world peace. Organize a youth rally for peace in the wake of a global crisis or conflict. Encourage your teenager to join a peace organization, to start a youth peace club at school, or to attend youth conferences on nonviolence. Teach your children that taking political action is a proud part of our heritage and that change only happens with engaged citizens.

• Hold fast to your deepest values and beliefs, even when positive change or world peace seems remote. In the end, children and adults must do our best to make a positive difference, and then we must let go and have faith in the potential power of love at work in the world.

Consider ten-year-old Rachel's call for a simple act of kindness: "What I really want that money can't buy is just one day where a smile isn't a rarity. Our world is becoming too cynical. You don't see many people smile or wave just to make someone happy. It would be so nice if one day you could make not just one person happy with a smile, but thirty. Then those thirty could bring happiness to thirty more. The nice thing about a smile is it doesn't cost anything, but is one of the most valuable things in the world. I would love to see just one day where a smile went a mile toward happiness in our world."

Lois, thirteen, took up a similar theme: "What do I really want that money can't buy? I could say world peace; I could say no more wars, no more drugs. But these are big things, things that do affect me, but don't, really. Not every day. . . .

"So what do I want? I want to be able to smile at any kid, no matter who they are, and have them smile back. Have them smile back not because of who I am, or what I look like, or where I am from, but just because I smiled at them.

"It is such a little thing, a smile. But if you smile, and someone smiles back, it makes you feel kind of silly, yet happy. It gives you a little warm feeling to know that you just exchanged smiles with someone for absolutely no reason. . . . It is the best because it relies on nothing else; it has no more or less meaning than that of two strange souls brushing against each other, only for a moment, but each of them leaving the other just a little better than they were before. . . . The only thing I can do is to dream, and keep smiling at the world. And maybe someday the world will smile back."

- Help your child to connect with other compassionate kids. Find a pen pal. This is a great way for kids to get to understand the life of someone living in a region of conflict, or a region with less material wealth than the United States. Various pen pal associations can provide an initial link. Consider going to World Pen-Pals, a global pen pal service; their web site is www.worldpen-pals.com. Children under thirteen years of age can safely search for similarly aged student pen pals throughout the world at the following web site: www.Ks-connection.org. American classrooms can get in

"Smile." Artist: Reiko

touch with classrooms overseas by going to www.epals.com.

- Teach your children to think about making the world a better place when they are planning their future careers. What better way to make the world a better place than to work at it full time? That won't be right for everyone, of course, but it should be something everyone factors into their decisions— jobs in the public or nonprofit sectors, targeting all kinds of issues. The *Washington Post* recently reported that 32 percent of college students nationwide are more interested in public service careers now than a year ago, compared with just 7 percent who are less interested, according to a survey by the consulting firm HotU Inc.

- Be a model for your children by taking political action, whether that means advocating for a conflict resolution curriculum in the school, writing to your representatives in support of global arms reduction, joining in demonstrations similar to the Million Mom March, or anything in between. Encourage your child to write a column for the school newspaper or start a new club at the school. Help your children make the connection between their own experiences and what happens in the world at large.

Too often we question our ability to solve the world's complex problems, turning inward and retreating from the civic sphere, believing ourselves incapable of tackling the tasks at hand. Given the scale and scope of our problems, this withdrawal is understandable, but the failure to act breeds cynicism and depression about the future. It may make us retreat into materialism. In contrast, youths who volunteer are 50 percent more likely to lead healthy, drug-free lives, according to the Search Institute. Volunteerism also improves children's self-esteem according to Susan Crites Price, author of *The Giving Family: Raising Our Children to Help Others.*

Our children want to feel genuine hope, excitement, and even anticipation about what tomorrow might bring—for them and for their own children. So be sure also to tell them the positive news that doesn't make headlines often enough, such as the fact that child literacy rates are up, teen pregnancy is down, population trends are stabilizing, many socially responsible corporations are producing environmentally friendly products from coffee to electric cars, the bald eagle no longer faces extinction, governments did tackle the ozone hole by negotiating an international treaty, and the international community is finally mobilizing to provide more debt relief and assistance to poor nations. Remind them that most of the big changes throughout history started with a small group of highly dedicated

"World Peace." Artist: Michael, age 14

people. Change is possible, and kids want it to happen. Surely this is one thing all parents can do to meet their children's nonmaterial needs. Using some of the tools in this chapter, your children will be able to follow their own best instincts as well.

## FOR FURTHER READING

*The Hero,* Ron Woods. New York, Alfred A. Knopf, 2002.
  (Inspirational fiction for the teen reader; especially appropriate for boys.)
*Miss Rumphius,* Barbara Cooney. New York, Viking Children's Books, 1982.
  (A read-aloud illustrated storybook for young children guaranteed to inspire both child and adult.)
*50 Simple Things Kids Can Do to Save the Earth,* Earth Works Group. Kansas

City, MO, Andres and McMeel, 1990.
(This book, available in most libraries, includes simple eco-friendly ideas for protecting the environment.)

## ADDITIONAL RESOURCES

Idealist.org for Kids, www.idealist.org/kat/aboutkt.html
(A positive web site started by kids, featuring local, national, and international volunteer efforts to make the world a better place.)
Teach for America, www.teachforamerica.org
(This nonprofit group places recent college graduates into public schools to teach in low-income communities.)
Habitat for Humanity, www.habitat.org
(Many high schools have Habitat for Humanity programs.)
Amnesty International, www.amnesty.org
(This international human rights organization has resources and programs for high school students.)
Environmental Career Opportunities, 6535 Broad Street, Bethesda, MD 20816, 1-800/315-9777, www.ecojobs.com
(An excellent bimonthly newsletter listing jobs as well as student internships with environmental groups and nature centers across the country.)
Opportunities in Public Affairs, 1-301-571-0102, www.brubach.com
(A bimonthly newsletter with postings on jobs and student internships in the public sector, with a primary focus on jobs in Washington, D.C., with the federal government or national nonprofit organizations.)
New Moon: The Magazine for Girls and their Dreams, www.newmoon.org
(A noncommercial magazine for adolescent girls.)

# Chapter 9

---

# Acceptance and Respect

*All I would ever want would be just for my family and friends to love me and accept me for who I am, not just what I look like, or what I have, I just want them to love me for me, and only me.*
—Ashleigh, 13

ALL HUMAN BEINGS have a strong need to be accepted by the group. Kids and teens especially have a powerful need to fit in, develop self-confidence, and know they are liked and respected. Sadly, advertisers and commercial forces relentlessly exploit this core need, with extraordinary costs to our kids. The entries we received on this topic are particularly poignant. With unflinching candor and insight, young people are literally crying out for a world that will value them for who they really are—rather than for what they look like, how well they dominate the pack, or what brand of products they can afford to purchase. A May 2001 *American Demographics* poll of kids ages seven to seventeen probed youth attitudes about popularity and possessions; one child in the poll summed up the major sentiment by sharing that "everything is judged by how much it was, how it looks on you, when and where you got it, and how many you have of it."

"Money Can't Buy… Respect." Artist: Stephanie S.

Acceptance is about connecting with the group and having a sense of belonging. Respect involves being recognized for achievement, talent, or character. Kids yearn for *authentic* feelings of connection, recognition, and power, yet teen culture assigns extraordinary importance to external appearances. Kids typecast each other as nerds, freaks, jocks, or preppies. Most teens feel pressure to dress, talk, and act in extremely specific ways—norms that are often defined and reinforced by the commercial media.

Here's how Tori, twelve, described the experience: "What I want that money can't buy is for everyone to be treated equally. I mean nowadays if you buy something at Wal-Mart you get made fun of, and that's just not right!! A lot of people get stuff from Abercrombie and American Eagle and the price is $30.00 for a shirt! Who cares? Don't treat us any different because we don't wear expensive name brand clothes!!"

Alison, thirteen, asserted: "The one thing I want that money can't buy is the feeling of being accepted. Without it you don't have the confidence to be yourself and with it you can do anything."

## BEING HAPPY WITH YOURSELF

Many kids wrote in about their desire for self-respect and self-love. Emily, thirteen, described it this way: "The thing that I want that money cannot buy would probably be to be happy with being myself because in this day and age it's pretty rare that people are truly happy with themselves. It's like everyone has to be super skinny, wear the right clothes, and hang with the 'popular' people to be considered cool; they just look at you and automatically judge you. I think a person should be happy with themselves because of what *they* think not what everyone else thinks. I mean, why should you have to live up to anyone else's expectations except your own? I mean, I know a lot of kids that aren't happy with themselves because they feel that they don't meet the right standards to be considered 'cool.' I know that at one point in time I wasn't too happy with myself because I did not think I was skinny enough and that I did not hang out with the right crowd, but then I just thought, why am I living up to what people want me to be? I want to be who I am, not like some doll that they mold me into."

Amy, sixteen, looks at it as a matter of self-esteem: "What I really want, not even Bill Gates' riches could buy. That is, completely healthy self-esteem, respect for others, and the motivation to attain both of these. . . . Most people tend to think that their self-esteem would be rejuvenated if they were zit-free, had the model body, and walked hand-in-hand with their dream date. In reality this approach is actually quite deceiving. I want to look at my reflection and only see happiness and security, instead of physical flaws. . . . Becoming and staying motivated to love oneself and others is hard work."

Bevin, seventeen, agrees that self-respect is the core issue: "If I could have anything I wanted that money could not buy, it would be self-respect. I believe that self-respect is a major thing that all kids need in their lives. It can determine how you live every day. It can affect the decisions you make and things you do. I feel that if someone does not have respect for himself that they will let other people over-take them and push them around. These people do not stand up for themselves and what they believe. They may be pressured into doing things they do not want to do. They could even turn to alcohol or get pressured into using drugs. These people will usually not have the future they would like to have because they do not believe in them-selves. They feel that they are not good enough to accomplish all of the things they dream of having. They will not work as hard and will settle for less their whole lives. . . . I hope I never lose the respect that I have for myself. I can walk down the halls at school and sense who has respect for themselves. . . . I feel that if you have no respect for your true self that you have nothing."

## FEELING ACCEPTED AND VALUED
## BY OTHERS

Many entrants revealed painful personal experiences stemming from social rejection or feelings of worthlessness. Serena, fifteen, wrote: "Wouldn't it be wonderful if people could just accept themselves as they are and be happy? The world would be free from eating disor-ders and diets would only be prescribed by doctors. The hovering black clouds of depression would give way to sunshine, and wrists would be slit-free. . . . I recently have won my personal battle with anorexia, and I am definitely much happier with myself. It hurts me terribly to see friends start down the same deadly road. They feel rejected by society because of their 'less than perfect bodies.' Occasionally, one of my girlfriends will find a boyfriend and snap out of the soon-to-be eating disorder. She no longer needs to diet as long as she feels truly loved by someone. It's a very sad thing when a girl feels so unloved that she will intentionally harm her body. . . . The world will truly be a better and more peaceful place for everyone if people could just accept themselves as they are and be happy."

## Knowing I'm Worth It

Some children, like Sarah, fifteen, are acutely aware of the struggle for self-acceptance:

As I walk into the ballet studio, I listen to my painfully skinny friends moan and groan, "Oh no, today's a fat day," . . . They stand in front of the all-too-revealing mirrors and examine their stomachs and thighs with all-too-critical eyes. Eyes shaped by boys, parents, and the media who told them they weren't good enough. . . .

The next day in health class, we learn about eating disorders. I numbingly take in the facts about anorexia and bulimia; I know they kill. Though it makes me so ashamed to admit it, in the back of my head, I still wish I had the self-control to put myself through that. Anything to achieve what society dictates to be beautiful.

Looking for a friend later on, I poke my head into the school weight room. I see a dozen guys straining themselves to lift barbells so large that the picture is almost ridiculous. As they grunt and sweat the pounds off, they think, "Maybe if I gain one more ounce of muscle, maybe if I can lift one more weight, maybe if I make my body ache just a little more, she will like me. Maybe then my friends will think I'm macho, and my father will believe I'm a man."

Then I go home. Another day has come to a close in the constant struggle to affirm my own sense of self. To love my body for what it is. To convince myself what my mother has always said, that inner beauty is more important. Deep down inside, I truly know I'm worth it. I know I'm intelligent, compassionate, and a good listener . . . but everything around me is telling me that looks are what really count. . . .

What do I want that money can't buy? I want to see a world where boys and girls can love their bodies for the beautiful and unique pieces of art that they are, without negative pressure coming from every direction. I want to see a world where media culture is a fair representation of real people. I want to see a world where no person is ashamed of looking the way they do. And most of all, I want to see a world where every boy and girl knows they are worth it.

## THE PROBLEM WITH "POPULAR" AND "COOL"

The social dynamics of early adolescence can even batter kids who have a strong sense of self. A study by psychologists at Hofstra University found that 100 percent of children had had the experience of being called hurtful names by other children. Almost all kids have had to deal with feelings of humiliation, rejection, and fear of being put down by their peers. The culture of "cool" exacerbates normal developmental pressures, leading kids to conform to very specific norms or face rejection and scorn.

It can get downright mean, overtly and physically as well as verbally and emotionally. Patrick, eleven, has been there: "One thing I really want that money can't buy is people in school to treat each other nicely and fairly. . . . In my middle school just about everyone teases and harasses people. Unfortunately I was considered a loser so that made me a major target for them. I never figured out what the difference between a 'loser' and a 'winner' was. They all thought they were big and tough and popular so they could push other people around and act important. Everybody called them the "Hockey

Crew" because they all played hockey together. . . . So what I want that money can't buy is for all bullies to know how that person feels when they are making fun of someone, then maybe they would stop."

This issue affects older teens and reaches down into elementary-school-age children as well. Listen to Keren, a fourth grader (and reformed culprit): "What do I want that money can't buy? I wish that the 'cooler' kids would stop making fun of the more helpless kids. I think that no one is better than anyone else. My fourth grade class had to read a book and do a report on that book. After I read my nonfiction book about Helen Keller and I saw how kids made fun of her because she was blind and deaf, it just made my heart drop. I realized that even though I made fun of people, for example, for how they dressed and knew it wasn't right, I did it anyway. I'm glad I stopped. In our school we have special needs classes. The kids in the classes are usually very young. Some of those kids may have Down's Syndrome or anything else. I hear kids in the older grades, third, fourth, and fifth, making fun of the other children. My friend Lauren and I and some other kids try to stop the kids from making fun of the special needs children."

Donald, ten, wrote on behalf of special needs kids: "What I want that money can't buy is to be normal like all of the other kids in school. I want to get a good education, I want to get equal rights, and I want to get out of the [special education] class. In the [special education] class I am called names, spitballs are thrown at me, and other kids are always fighting about something, but most of all I don't feel normal. That is why I'm mainstreaming out of the [special education] class."

Many kids also wrote in about not being accepted because of the color of their skin. Racial and ethnic differences continue to divide kids and adults despite heartfelt yearnings for a color-blind world. Take Jin, age seventeen: "I would like the chance to see the day when racial issues disappear forever. The day when people of different colors can become friends without the hassles which seem to come along with it. The day when various races live together with a common goal—to make this place the best place to live. The day when some-

"Friendship between peoples of different colors, race, & religion." Artist: Araceli, age 12

one first sees a person as a potential friend, rather than a target. The day when one becomes able to judge someone by their personality, rather than their appearance." Children from minority racial and ethnic groups often start out feeling excluded from the mainstream, and their struggle for acceptance and respect can be especially complex.

Few kids escape the tribulations of peer pressure or feelings of at least temporary exclusion from the group. Kids must find their place in the social hierarchy, and it's hard to do that smoothly when their bodies are changing, their emotions are in flux, they're shifting to new school settings, and they're bombarded with media messages amplifying the problem. No wonder many parents worry about whether their kids are fitting in, finding the right friends, and developing appropriate levels of self-confidence.

# WHAT CAN PARENTS DO?

Adults have always played an important role in helping kids find their way from childhood to young adulthood. In traditional Native American culture, it was the duty of all adults to serve as teachers for young people. Today, parents tend to be more alone, although if you're lucky, other family members, neighbors, and teachers can play supporting roles.

## Show Them Your Love

The first step is the most obvious: Help your child feel worthy by loving her unconditionally—when she succeeds *and* when she fails. Clinical psychologist Alan Davidson noted in *How Good Parents Raise Great Kids,* "For children to feel good about themselves, parents must feel good about them first." One of the challenges of modern parenting is that we want our children to have high aspirations and to succeed in life, but we also want them to like themselves the way they are. Not everyone can be number one, and we have to let our children know that we love them even when they're not king of the mountain. Acknowledge their small achievements, notice their efforts to be independent, and offer them encouragement especially when they're feeling down about themselves. Even when your love can't solve their feelings of rejection or self-doubt, it always helps, and it keeps kids anchored in the midst of their social storms.

Erika, fourteen, summed it up: "What I really want that money can't buy is unconditional love. As a kid, I need to know that no matter what happens, no matter what grades I get—I will be loved." Fifteen-year-old Joe spelled it out this way: "What I really want that money can't buy is someone that cares about me and loves me and that will take care of me no matter what happens. Someone who is willing to help me and be there for me even if I choose to do the wrong things in life. Someone that is not mean, inconsiderate, or that lies to me."

## Distinguish Popularity from Authentic Friendship

Parents can help kids understand the difference between popularity and friendship. Popularity is elusive, yet every child wants it. From a kid's perspective, being popular means you are okay; you're somebody. To be ignored or rejected means you're nobody. According to research at Duke University, only 15 percent of kids are considered popular in any given school, although many more are "accepted." Popularity is what kids focus on, but friends are what they ultimately need. Christopher, thirteen, struggled to fit in and finally found his way through good friendships: "What I really want that money can't buy is acceptance. I know what it feels like to be on the other side, a dork, a dweeb, you get the picture, right? Well, I'll tell you what, I would have done close to anything to just have one of those popular people say 'hi' to me, or even just glance at me, as long as I was noticed. Without the feeling of acceptance from your peers, your life seems dull and stupid because you don't have anyone to tell about 'what happened at lunch' or 'what you did over the holidays.' Believe me, the only way you can truly be accepted would be to be self-confident. Many kids feel so unaccepted that they turn to razor blades, drinking, drugs, and even suicide, but you can turn that around if you stop worrying about what they might say about you, but what you say about yourself. I used to be unaccepted, but now I am living happily with many friends, and my whole life is ahead of me."

Malinda, fourteen, feels the same urgency for having a clear place for herself in the world, and she has found solace in friendship: "The one thing in the world that I want most is the sense of belonging. To have friends and family that are supportive and caring gives me the greatest feeling. Having people to laugh and cry with means a lot during hard times, and being able to make and share memories with someone makes me feel important. My family has always and always will be supportive and caring to me, but it is hard to come by friends that can give me the same feeling. So many people in the world today judge and make fun of other people; they make it hard for me to find someone not like that. A friend that makes me feel as if

I belong is someone who judges no one, someone who lets me be who I really am, and someone who goes beyond the outside appearance of a person to find their inner beauty. . . . Without a group of people to *belong* to, I feel alone and jealous of everyone else with close friends. . . . I will rely on my family, friends I have now, and friends I hope to make in the future to support me and give me a sense of belonging. I will in return do the same to them."

## Talk about It

Communication between parent and child is, as always, key. It's important to look beyond surface behavior to grasp what's really going on. Try to find out where your child fits in his social milieu. Talk to teachers, observe your child with other kids, take notice of whether your child has friends, attends parties, gets phone calls, and wants to be with other children. Many young people feel alienated and isolated. Almost all have had to cope with insults, verbal put-downs, and feelings of rejection. Talk about similar problems you had at their age. Explain the unreliability of cliques and the importance of being a good, trustworthy friend. Encourage your children to seek out friends with similar interests and values. This level of empathy and sharing can help your kids know that there is a light at the end of their social tunnel.

In my family, the most effective communication on this issue came not from us as parents, but from an older teenager who is a family friend (and whom my daughter considers both "nice" and "cool"). In middle school my daughter was briefly afflicted with self-doubt, feeling she didn't fit in, and struggling to find a close friend. This older girl told my daughter about how she'd gone through similar rough times at that same middle school. She was extremely reassuring, saying that by ninth grade, kids have a better sense of what they really care about and as a result, the pressure eases as everyone finds their niche. Nothing I could say or do hit home like this personal testimony from someone who really knew both how painful it could be and that there was a pathway through it. The affirmation and empathy of a slightly older child can be reassuring. My daughter got that particular boost by chance, but if I had known how effective it would be, I would have tried to engineer the circumstances myself!

## Teach Self-Reliance and Perseverance

Ultimately, respect and feelings of self-worth require more than parental love. They must be earned. Sometimes, as parents, we get so anxious about our children that we praise them excessively or pamper and overprotect them. This path is well intentioned but rarely results in a happy child with high self-esteem. Perhaps we get overly involved because we worry about the extremely competitive turf of modern childhood. Perhaps we are too invested in the results of their efforts and not focused sufficiently on helping them develop the lifelong tools of persistence, perseverance, and determination, traits typically developed in the aftermath of mistakes or rejection. If kids want and need real respect and acceptance, they must earn it.

Meeting a challenge or fulfilling a goal inspires pride, confidence, and self-worth based not on superficial measures but on real ways of being in the world. For Megan, fifteen, this means being the best swimmer she can be: "Imagine! The stands are full of hundreds of excited fans cheering and encouraging me on. It's the final lap, and I am neck to neck with another swimmer. Every inch of my body is in extreme pain, but I gather all of my inner strength and win the race by one second. Winning that race is the one thing I want that money cannot buy. The only way I can accomplish this is by practicing, believing in myself, and trying the best that I can. . . . The only way that I can become a stronger swimmer than I was before is by hard work and long hours of training. I know it may be hard, but the joy of knowing that I won and that I did it all by myself is well worth it in the end. . . . In order to win that race, it is essential that I have enough confidence in my performance and me. . . . I would rather lose the swim meet and had given it my best instead of winning it and not even have tried at all."

"Guitar Virtuoso." Artist: Caroline, age 14

Twelve-year-old Brittany found the same satisfaction by improving her riding skills: ". . . PERSISTENCE. You can't buy it from a store or borrow it from a friend or order it from a catalog. . . . But many times I sure wished I had a big dose of it in a jar or something. I would drink it down like a shake and presto I'm feeling good and I'm persistent and unstoppable in my thoughts and actions. I want to be a professional show jumping rider. . . . Even though I've been told that I have a natural gift for riding, it won't get me anywhere unless I am PERSISTENT with my practices, schooling, and showing. I have to be persistent about spending my time wisely, taking advantage of opportunities that come my way, and sometimes even make my own opportunities and luck. Unless I keep my eyes on my goals, my dreams won't come true."

The key to helping your children in this area is all in how you define achievement. We should encourage and celebrate mastery, even of more modest tasks. Since not everyone is going to win the science fair or place first at the recital, it is the smaller, more personal achievements that really bring the big rewards. Help your younger children achieve successes that are within their capabilities. This will convince them that they can do things well. Help your older children get involved in athletic, artistic, community, or academic ventures in which they have a latent talent or interest.

Praise your children for their persistence, practice, and efforts as well as their eventual success. Teach them to handle the inevitable frustration productively—rather than just quit when they hit a wall. Remind them that the people who have the patience to climb *and* fall make progress toward their personal goals. Encourage them to read books about achievers who had to struggle for success: Helen Keller, Frederick Douglass, and Albert Einstein, to name a few.

## Increase Freedom—and Responsibility

You should also provide what growing kids are yearning for: increased freedom. Remember to emphasize that freedom must go hand in hand with increased responsibility as well. You might think this would be a natural lesson to teach, yet we parents in today's complex world have two tendencies that get in the way: The first is overprotection; the second is pushing children too hard or too fast. They are conflicting impulses, I know, but they both arise out of our reaction to the sometimes scary world out there—and our deep love for our children. We get mixed signals: "Protect your kids; the world isn't safe" versus "Equip your kids; the world isn't safe."

In some cases our kids benefit from stretching, but often we are overloading them. Pushed out too far and too fast, kids can get fearful, discouraged, and burned out. Instead of gaining confidence and self-reliance, they actually lose it. On the other hand, sometimes we worry so much about our kids that we get overly involved and try to orchestrate all the details of their lives, not allowing them to make

"PRIDE." Artist: Blake

mistakes or cope with inevitable disappointments. When this protec-
tiveness goes completely awry, we end up with so-called "spoiled"
kids. A recent Time/CNN poll showed that 68 percent of parents said
their own children are "very" or "somewhat" spoiled. Another survey
pointed out that 80 percent of people think kids are more spoiled
now than they were ten or fifteen years ago—with two thirds admit-
ting their own children are spoiled.

When we intervene to keep our children from making mistakes,
we are depriving them of opportunities for growth and self-reliance.
This may not be "spoiling" in the traditional sense, but it can under-
mine a child's independence and self-respect—something kids say
they want. Parents have to learn to let go, while helping kids know
they are loved.

In giving more freedom, ask for more help. On the most basic
level, that means children should take on some household chores,
with increasing duties as they get older. Parenting experts Foster
Cline and Jim Fay stress that helping with housework develops self-
worth and enhances the child's feelings of being part of a team.
Encourage your children's efforts by making positive comments about
how well they've done their chores.

Kids want to feel useful (don't we all?). So teach them how to
be. They want to know their lives have external value, and that starts
in these most basic ways. Your children depend on you; let them
know you depend on them as well—and let them show you that they
can be depended on.

## Compromise Sometimes

Your kids may well hear and understand your analysis, may feel your
love and respect, yet they may still be troubled by the pressure to buy
into all parts of teen culture. This pressure is real, so don't dismiss it.

The bell rings and all of a sudden the hall gets crowded. I walk past each person, being pushed trying to reach my destination, my next class, and see the new kid with a hip new North Face book bag and everybody liking him for the day. At the end of the hall, a girl has the new Phat Farm jacket, and many other girls stare at it with admiration. This is what life is like for the typical teenage boy or girl—a time full of self-consciousness, school stress, popularity contests, peer pressure . . .

I, myself, feel as if I have never actually known who I am, and I'm still trying to figure it out. Nowadays, people are defined by the school they go to. When people ask me where I go to school and when I answer them Junior High School 189, they automatically think that I'm bad. They think that because many kids outside hear many rumors of all the bad things that have happened in our school, but nobody spreads around what good has happened in our school. Also, there is so much pressure that is put on us because we have to choose what school we should go to next. I have to think if I should try for a specialized high school and study so much. If I don't get in, what am I going to do? Will everyone think I'm dumb? . . .

My first day of school, I walked in and saw all the different kids that I'm going to stay with for two or three years. I saw them looking at each other's clothes and complimenting each other. I felt as if all they thought of was trying to be popular or fitting in and some people checking in their little pocket mirrors seeing if they are looking fine. Then the next day, I see all these girls trying to help each other out to be pretty and popular by fixing them up with makeup and expensive clothing. I hear girls thinking that they're ugly because a guy doesn't like her. I don't understand how someone else thinking they are pretty magically makes them that way. I feel as if the self-consciousness in our school is too high. . . .

My parents don't know what I want. Sometimes I want to go out, but they don't let me and they keep me captive in my room. . . . One time, my friend invited me to go to the mall, but they didn't let me go. I didn't talk to them for a week. Even if I had gone to the mall, it's not like I could have bought the perfect teenage years off the shelf. I know this is the time that I'm supposed to learn a lot about myself, but I wish I could learn without going through popularity contests and the everyday stress of an adolescent . . .

—Ephraim, 12

Sometimes the stress gets too high, and it requires compromise by both kids and parents. Children who suffer group rejection must cope with teasing, name-calling, exclusion, and sometimes bullying. If your child is in this situation and her feelings of self-worth are low, do get involved. If you feel you are giving love, authentic praise, and opportunities for independence yet something still seems amiss, look deeper. Maybe she needs help conforming to some group norms. Sometimes it's important that you help your child have the safety of the right "look." On a simple level, this may require some parental compromise—including the purchase of something you'd really rather not buy. Still, the compromise runs both ways. In no way should you try to buy your child's way to popularity. It just can't be done. Parents may need to provide some of the surface goods that help kids feel they're "okay," but kids need to also know that parents can't and won't buy them all the brand-name goods that kids are made to feel they *must* have. This is the dance—helping them fit in but resisting efforts to buy their way into popularity or coolness.

Of course, when signs of depression, isolation, and anger persist, no small purchase will fix the problem. If your child is being rejected not just by one or two children but by the entire group, seek help. Speak with a school counselor, teachers, and neighbors if appropriate. Feelings of low self-esteem and social rejection are cause for concern. A report on youth self-esteem by the state of California, led by Assemblyman John Vasconcellos, concluded that "Self-esteem is something that empowers us to live responsibly and that inoculates us against the lures of crime, violence, and substance abuse, chronic welfare dependency, and educational failure." Many argue that the core cause of violence in our society stems from feelings of isolation and social rejection. A study by the Los Angeles Police Department links low feelings of acceptance and respect with growing gang activity in schools nationwide.

## Expect Tough Times

Expect some tough times as your children struggle to grow up. Expect the turbulence, often peaking in the early teenage years. Your challenge is to support their newfound independence while helping them remain emotionally connected to family. This is a normal developmental stage, yet nowadays it is also cultural combat. Anticipating the social turmoil and adolescent struggle for an authentic identity helps. Talking about it and knowing you will pull through it can be very helpful in getting both parents and kids through the rough spots. In her book *Reviving Ophelia,* noted family therapist Mary Pipher writes about the self-doubt and anxiety young teens almost universally experience: "It's not a fatal disease, but an acute condition that disappears with time. While it's happening, nobody looks strong."

### Knowing I Do Fit In

The single thing I have always wanted which money could never buy me was the understanding of whom I was and where I fit in. The moment that I stepped into my kindergarten class, the realization that I was different hit me hard and brought me to tears. My lack of skills in the English language caused me to almost fail all of the standardized tests issued the first several years of school. Against the recommendations of my teachers, my parents pushed me on, with the sheer sliver of hope that I would prevail.

Their confidence in me was the backbone of my character, as I learned to deal with my differences from all of my "all-American" peers. My mother carried a thick accent with her and looked different from all the other mothers. English was not spoken at my home, and all of my clothing came from Europe. When others spoke of their vacations to the Jersey Shore and Disney World, I shared my stories of summer in Portugal.

My immaturity made it difficult to be different. I longed to change my name and forget that any of my roots were in Portugal. As my age increased, so did my views. I realized that I was blessed to know a second language from birth, to be given the pleasure to travel the wonders of Western Europe, and to understand the different ways of life known around the world. I was one of the few who understood that America was not the world.

I blossomed in high school. People complimented my name and envied the fact that I was fluent in a beautiful language. I began to find myself and came to realize that my disparate background was an asset, not a burden. Finally, I understood, there is no prototypical all-American. Rather, it is composed of the differences among us, the ones that form our individuality and very distinct identities, melded from a beautiful, encompassing ideal."

—Mei-Li, 17

## Mark Rites of Passage

Formally acknowledging the transition into adulthood—or at least the beginning of the transition—is an excellent way to reinforce self-esteem and self-reliance, and also acceptance into a wider community. I don't come from the Jewish tradition, but I've often longed for something similar to a bar or bat mitzvah in my family. I particularly value the Jewish ceremonies that give children a chance to study and reflect on important matters and to be surrounded and supported by community and affirmed by elders and peers. It is a time to stand back and celebrate how one child is becoming a full, free person. This type of special event, perhaps in conjunction with a birthday, can offer an opportunity to affirm and offer support to a developing teenager.

All kids want the love and affirmation of those they love the most. As Melek, eleven, said: "The one thing that I want is love. Love from my family, and love from the people who know me best. I want to be trusted and well known because of the goodness of my heart. I want my family to love me for who I am, and how I act. I want to be loved by everyone who knows me because I am respectful. People who know me know that I am responsible, and I want to be respected for that. I want my family to know me; I want them to love the me that they know."

## Connect Your Kids with Something More than the Self

Many of the other chapters in this book also help point the way to self-respect and ultimately respect from others. When your child embarks on a spiritual journey or decides to do something to make the world a better place, he is building self-respect and often is winning approval from his group. Help your child do something positive for someone else. This is one of the best ways to counter the low self-esteem and to earn both acceptance and respect from others.

I want a world where I can just be me. Plain and simple. It sounds like a given, but it's not. We live in a world where we, as children, are not allowed the time it takes to find out who we are. We live in a society that tells us who we have to be and how we have to act if we are to "get ahead." . . . Early on we learn that if we don't conform in dress, speech, and mannerisms, we will not fit in with the "cool kids." As teens if we don't have a car, we might as well be lepers. If we aren't good at sports, if we don't make good grades, if we don't score high enough on the SATs, and if we don't get into the "right" college, we are seen as failures by our coaches, teachers, and in some instances even by our own parents. If guys aren't athletic and handsome and if girls aren't thin and beautiful, like the ads on TV dictate, we soon begin to think we are without value. . . .

I don't want to play the game and pretend to be someone that I am not. I don't want to have to adjust who I am depending on who I am with. I want time to figure out who I really am, what I think, what I believe, and what I feel. . . . I don't want to have to compete and be compared to someone else in order to obtain a relative degree of success on some capricious scale. Bottom line: I don't want to have to commit emotional and psychological suicide to be considered successful. I just want to be me. . . .

I want to live in a world where who I am matters more than what I am. . . . I want to live in a world where success is a subjective state of being and must begin with a realization of who you are—the inside you—and what makes you really happy.

I want to live in a world where . . . the climb to success begins with a descent into the depth of our souls. Here we must learn to recognize, appreciate, and begin building on the bedrock of our good qualities. Here we must learn to recognize, confront, and begin modifying our bad qualities. Only when we really know who we are and what makes us tick can we begin the climb from the inside out. The ascent is an unending process, yet this is success. And this is what I want for all of us: not to reach perfection but to be who we are and to be the best "who" we can be while living happily in harmony with the creation around us and making a positive difference in the lives of others.

I just want to be me. In the land of liberty, is that too much to ask?

—Jason, 13

# FOR FURTHER READING

*The Girl Pages: A Handbook of the Best Resources for Strong, Confident, Creative Girls,* Charlotte Milholland. New York, Hyperion Press, 1998.
(An excellent compendium of books, videos, web sites, summer camps, and other resources for building the esteem and confidence of adolescent girls.)

*Real Boys: Rescuing Our Sons from the Myths of Boyhood,* William Pollack. Carlton, Victoria, Australia, Scribe Publications, 1999. Released in the U.S.A. by Henry Holt, New York.

*Handbook for Boys: A Novel,* Walter Dean Myers. New York, HarperCollins, 2002.

*Reviving Ophelia: Saving the Selves of Adolescent Girls,* Mary Pipher, Ph.D. New York, Ballantine Books, 1994.
(An outstanding book for parents of adolescent girls who have concerns about the cultural pressures that force girls to suppress their true identities and conform to negative cultural archetypes and norms.)

*How Good Parents Raise Great Kids,* Alan Davidson and Robert Davidson. New York, Warner Books, 1996.

*The Measure of Our Success,* Marian Wright Edelman. New York: HarperPerennial, 1992.

*Stopping at Every Lemonade Stand,* James Vollbracht. New York: Penguin USA, 2001.

# Chapter 10

# Health

*What I really want that money can't buy is to always be healthy and energetic. I could play every day and go to school to get a good education. Also I wouldn't get sick a lot.*
—Nicholas, 4th grade

KIDS OFTEN ASSUME they are invulnerable and their lives eternal, yet a surprising number of contest entries expressed health concerns about smoking, drugs, and alcohol, as well as about serious illnesses and chronic health conditions. Parents worry about these same issues—with good cause. To name just a few examples: After a few years of declining illicit drug use, the use of drugs such as marijuana, uppers, and heroin rose among high school seniors during the 2000–01 school year, according to PrideSurveys.com. A Harvard University study reports that children as young as nine are taking up cigarettes—in an attempt to control their weight! Childhood obesity is rising rapidly. Ironically, eating disorders are also on the rise, affecting five to ten million Americans a year. Eighty-one percent of *ten-year-olds* are afraid of being fat, and just over half of nine- and ten-year-old girls say they feel better about themselves when they are dieting.

There are bright spots, including declines in teenage pregnancy rates and cigarette smoking, but we still have concerns (sexual activity is starting younger and younger). The number of young people who drink alcohol and smoke cigarettes dipped to the lowest point in thirteen years in 2001, yet 31 percent of high school students binge drink, and alcohol-related automobile accidents involving teens have risen (PrideSurveys.com).

Children also must cope with more serious health problems that are often beyond any parent's control. Childhood asthma and allergies have risen dramatically, with most medical experts attributing these trends to environmental factors. Far too many children confront life-threatening diseases such as cancer, while others suffer from autism, muscular dystrophy, and other illnesses. The children who wrote in about these more difficult situations were passionate and extremely clear about what mattered to them. I have included some of their moving excerpts in part to remind all of us to treasure our nonmaterial gifts, especially the gift of health.

Parents can help their children get off to a healthy start and develop lifelong habits to foster good living. This chapter helps you start that journey by looking at diet, exercise, sleep, safety, and addictions including smoking, drugs, and alcohol, and what you can do to guide your children to a healthy lifestyle.

Kids understand the importance of starting out right. Take Gillian, ten, for example:

Money can buy tools and food you need, but it can't buy good health. I think this is important because you need to have good health if you want to live. If you smoke or get drunk, you should try to stop before you ruin your health. You know all the money in the world can't cure lung cancer, and you can't undo the damage if you're injured in a drunk driving accident. If you have good health, you can run around, have fun, and do lots of fun things. If you have good health, you can be a better parent and not teach your kids to have bad health, too. So remember that money can't buy good health, and without good health, what good is money?

Many of the health issues facing young people and adults are connected in some way to our out-of-whack culture. Take our pervasive problems with dieting for example. Are Americans disproportionately overweight because of flaws in our characters? I don't think so. We are operating in a culture that, on multiple dimensions, propels many of us—kids and adults alike—to gain unwanted pounds. Exercise time is limited, while stress (a leading cause of overeating) is epidemic. Schools have cut back on physical education, often in an effort to cram in sufficient time for the increasing number of standardized tests or more academic subjects. We leave little time for food preparation, so we eat fast food, which is almost universally high in fat and low in nutrients. Our leisure time is overwhelmingly spent at sedentary pastimes having to do with commercial and electronic products. "More is better" is apt for describing what's happened to food portions, with the average size of sodas, bagels, candy bars, and restaurant servings surging. And there is growing evidence from eating disorder experts that millions of Americans are eating in an attempt to fulfill unmet nonmaterial needs—for example, for companionship, love, or a sense of purpose in life.

The incidence of high cholesterol and diabetes, and increased risk for developing myriad diseases in adulthood, has risen dramatically among children, largely due to an epidemic of childhood obesity. This is how Crystal, sixteen, has experienced it: "The one thing in the world that I want more than anything that money can't buy, is a cure for . . . diabetes. My eight-year-old brother has this disease, and it stops him from doing all the things a normal kid can do."

The percentage of overweight children ages six to eleven has almost doubled since 1970, from 7 to 13 percent. For teens the news is even worse, with rates tripling from 5 to 14 percent. (And those numbers just keep on growing over the years—half of American adults are overweight, and one in four is obese.) Rates of type II diabetes, which is weight related, have increased more than fourfold among children over the last twenty years.

The good news is that all the steps you are taking with this book to meet your children's deeper needs will support their physical and mental health. As their nonmaterial needs are more fully met, they will be that much less likely to try to fill their empty places with unhealthy bad habits.

## TAMING OUR FOOD HABITS

Ultimately, kids must take responsibility for their own nutrition. But they can't do it all on their own. It helps when parents model healthy behavior. (Or when our behavior is not healthy, it helps if we at least acknowledge our shortcomings and intentions to change.) Kids also need us to teach and support them, establishing healthful habits within our homes and families. We've got a lot of work to do: USDA statistics show that Americans' total daily caloric intake has risen from 1,854 calories to 2,002 calories over the last twenty years. That significant increase—148 calories per day—theoretically works out to an extra fifteen pounds every year!

Here are a few basic strategies to get you started toward healthier eating habits:

- It is never too late to establish good eating habits—for yourself as well as for your children. For many people, this has less to do with the details of any specific nutritional approach and more to do with slowing down enough to pay attention and change habits. Regardless of all the tabloid advice, eating well is not rocket science. Limit high-sugar and high-fat foods while maximizing physical activity. For many, this commonsense change is much easier when simultaneously taken with steps to reduce stress. When we are exhausted, isolated, or depressed, it's too easy to grab for food as a source of comfort. Our kids can fall into the same trap.
- Provide a balanced diet. Serve a wide variety of healthful foods. As much as possible, steer clear of processed foods, which are low in nutrition anyway and also are major contributors to longer-term health problems. Try to do what we all

know we should do: eat more fruits and vegetables; eat unrefined grains; eat fewer saturated animal fats and more unsaturated vegetable oils; and eat less meat, white flour, and sugar. For working parents, this can be a challenge, but a growing number of cookbooks offer recipes for easy, nutritious, delicious meals. Whether bean enchiladas or homemade pita bread veggie pizzas, there are plenty of recipes to be found that are healthy, that your kids will like, and that don't require a gourmet cook in the kitchen!

- Keep an eye on portions. Many restaurants feature "all you can eat" or "free refills," and nearly all of them serve up monstrous portions, and we tend to follow suit at home. The standard size restaurant plate has increased from ten to twelve inches to accommodate the increases. The largest size of McDonald's French fries *is* three times larger than that of a generation ago. Think for just a minute about the whole concept of "The Big Gulp." The typical soda was eight ounces in the late 1950s, while today's "large" is closer to thirty-two ounces (also known as a quart!). Studies show that the average person (child or adult) will describe a "regular" muffin as two, three, or even four times the size the federal government uses as the basis of food recommendations. When you serve meals to your family, start with modest portions and eat slowly.

- Make healthy snacks available. After-school snacks are particularly key—most kids are starving when they walk in the door. Have good choices on hand, and make sure your children know the options so they won't just run out to the nearest candy store. It sometimes feels like an uphill battle with all the pressure to buy chips, cookies, and junk food. Try shifting to fruits, baby carrots, vanilla yogurt, or any number of alternatives to packaged or processed food. A tray of cut-up raw vegetables in the refrigerator *is* something kids will reach for if you remove snack chips and cookies from the cupboards.

- Teach your children early about being responsible food consumers. For my family, that means buying local and organic as much as possible, washing all fruits and vegetables thoroughly, and looking for food products that are produced in socially responsible ways. I worry about food safety, as every parent must. The science on what is safe keeps changing. The best thing to do is to train your kids (and yourself!) to keep asking, What's in it? Who made it? Where does it come from? It's sometimes hard to sort out the facts from fiction, but asking questions is a key part of being a healthy, wise consumer. In general, look for the organic and fair trade labels and be part of the growing movement of consumers who are making our food safer and healthier for the environment too.
- Look at what is happening at school. Lunch programs at public schools were designed to provide good nutrition, especially to underprivileged children. Yet nowadays, menu options typically include fast food pizza or a burger any day, and that's exactly what most kids dine on in school—every day. The other choice is supposedly a balanced plate of meat, starch, and vegetable, but the protein is nearly always fried or doused in fatty cheese and dwarfs the serving size of the vegetables (which are so unappealingly prepared I wouldn't eat them either). The top three foods sold in schools today are potato chips, tortilla chips, and cookies. Soda tops the list of beverages sold at school, beating out milk by a long shot.

  That's not to mention the vending machines dispensing sodas and snacks in schools. There's no need to even go as far as the cafeteria for your breakfast or lunch! No wonder kids today drink more soda than water. Many schools have contracts with soda companies that include financial incentives for the schools to *increase* student consumption of soda. Before the epidemic of childhood obesity will end, the school system will have to change. Parents—organized parents who speak up—can make a difference. Most menus are decided at the county level, where parents can make themselves heard. Policy about vending machines is often set at the school level, and is even more open to parental input.

- Get your kids involved in growing and preparing food. It's remarkable how many children have no idea where their food comes from. Try helping your child to grow something—a potted tomato or cucumber or a small garden patch of vegetables and berries. What kids grow, they tend to eat.

- Beware of the culture of obsessive thinness. Fear of fat is the other side of the overeating epidemic. There are shelves of books on this issue, but the bottom line is that preaching to your kids about staying thin, dieting, and watching their weight can lead to serious eating disorders and, in extreme cases, can jeopardize their well-being. The point of eating healthfully is to be healthy—not to be thin.

- Think about what we are eating *for.* A lot of different dynamics may underlie this simple question. Very rarely is the answer just, I'm eating because I am hungry. Not all of those dynamics are necessarily bad. But too often eating is just one more way to try to meet a nonmaterial need in a material way. Dozens of social science studies have demonstrated a connection between various eating disorders and unmet emotional needs. Research shows that the real need will never be met with substitutes. (The same holds for smoking, drinking, drugs, and premature sexuality as well.) Putting the emphasis on meeting nonmaterial needs in appropriate nonmaterial ways helps kids (and adults) say no to the unhealthy things pushed at us all the time—including too much food.

## EXERCISE

The advice for exercise is similar to the advice for eating habits: Set an example, look at your own habits, establish good habits for your kids, look at what is happening at school—but don't go so far as to create obsessive exercisers bent on thinness at all costs.

The data on how sedentary children have become are discouraging. We are raising a generation of "tele-chubbies." In a study released by the *Journal of the American Medical Association*, researchers at Stanford University demonstrated a direct link between watching television and body weight. Nielsen Media Research indicates that children typically spend nearly four hours a day in front of the set.

For all the recent growth of youth sports leagues, on average kids are getting far less exercise than they used to. Schools across the country have cut way back on PE, and many have even stopped or greatly reduced recess. When my kids were nine and ten years old, they got just fifteen minutes a day of recess.

Less than a third of Americans get the minimum amount of exercise medical experts recommend. Furthermore, the sports leagues and school teams that are the major outlet for children's physical activity these days tend to be highly competitive. That's a good fit for some kids, but it puts others off. Many children quickly come to feel they are not good enough if they are not going to be superstars. When they pull out, there aren't many other organized, supervised options for them.

As with any aspect of health, especially with mixed messages coming from the schools and the culture at large, your kids need you to communicate clearly with them about the importance of exercise to their current and long-term health. The key to having naturally active children, however, is in making exercise fun. Part of that is finding options that are right for your particular child. Different kids have different passions. So find something (or some things) that works for your kid, be it biking, hiking, regular playground excursions, dancing freestyle to his or her favorite music, or anything else.

You and your children can do many types of exercise together, which will grant their wish for more time with you! Adults need to be exercising more too, and kids sometimes worry about others' health more than they do about their own. But you should also make it easy for your kids to exercise independently. Ultimately, it isn't going to be your job to keep them healthy over their lifetimes—they have to take ownership of their own health. The more you all discover the fun in physical activity, the more likely you'll all be to make it a lifelong habit.

## ADDICTIONS

When it comes to alcohol, drugs, and smoking, don't assume that the schools are taking care of this education for you. Social science shows that parents have the most influence anyway. So give your kids a kind of psychological vaccination, and don't wait until they are teenagers to do it (although regular "booster shots" are definitely indicated). Most schools start education about addictions with fourth or fifth graders, when the kids can fully understand, are probably starting to observe closely what older kids do, and are still young enough to hear messages from authority figures while keeping an open mind. What exactly you cover, and how, should of course be determined by you and will change according to your child's age and life experiences.

Share the potential dangers that concern you. Don't evoke fear or dread, but do emphasize legitimate caution. Talk about what addiction is, and how powerful it is. We all (and especially kids) like to experiment—seeking out novelty is part of human nature. If the family knows someone with an addiction, consider talking about the person's experiences and problems, including his or her desire to stop smoking or drinking. Personal stories always help kids to "get it."

Amanda, thirteen, already knows the dangers of smoking: "A few years ago my grandfather died at the age of sixty-one after suffering a stroke and a heart attack. He had been a diabetic and was a long-term heavy smoker. The doctors said he was a 'walking time bomb.'. . . Money definitely cannot buy the one thing that I long for; I don't want my father to face the health problems my grandfather experienced. My father is also addicted to cigarettes. I am very close to my family, and I love my dad so much. I couldn't bear to see anything terrible happen to him, especially if it's caused by a bad habit. . . . I want my dad to be alive for the special moments of my life."

Audra, twelve, has had a different but equally distressing experience: "What I really want that money can't buy is for me, my brother, my mom, and my dad to be a family again. I think part of the problem is that he has a bad smoking and drinking problem. It's not that my dad is a bad person; actually he is a wonderful person who loves his children more than anything in the whole world. I know that for a fact."

Amanda and Audra remind us of the huge risks involved with our own addictive problems. We all know that these addictions are powerful, and most medical professionals view them as biochemical illnesses. Often, to conquer their hold on us, we need support. Seek help if you have had trouble with alcohol, drugs, or cigarettes. Your efforts to fight back against these diseases, even if the going is tough, will mean so much to your kids.

Many kids are very concerned about others. Beata, a seventh grader, wrote: "The thing that I would want that money couldn't buy is for my brother to stop smoking. . . . I don't want him to get lung cancer, or for him to die at an early age. I would also want his girlfriend, Heather, to stop smoking too. I hear on the news and from people that so many people get cancer from smoking or die from smoking. It is even more dangerous for the people who don't smoke but live with someone who smokes and have to breathe in the smoke. The reason for that is because smokers have a filter on their cigarettes, so the filter absorbs or captures most of the poison. The people who have to breathe in the smoke automatically breathe in the poisons from the cigarette."

Anne, age nine, wrote of her extended family's painful experience with alcohol abuse: "What I want that money can't buy would be that all the alcohol would be destroyed and that it never even came into the world. My aunt died by using alcohol. I feel bad for her. What about all the other people? People in the world die every day from having alcohol in their systems. It makes people crazy and I don't like it, I HATE IT! . . . Money can't buy that, and people can't stop them. People are wasting money, hurting their families, and hurting themselves. I wish it would stop, I really do."

## SLEEP

We're not getting enough sleep—not young children, not teenagers, not their parents. A recent poll by the National Sleep Foundation revealed that a majority of Americans say they do not get the eight hours of sleep each night recommended for most adults. And without enough sleep, our health suffers. Beyond that, we're just plain tired too much of the time! Only an estimated 15 percent of high school students get the recommended hours of sleep each night. Kids come home from school exhausted, and lack of sleep, rather than mental exertion, is a large part of the reason. Teenagers especially tend to flop down on the couch every chance they get.

The kids themselves are asking for a change. Here's Ross, twelve: "[I want] . . . middle school and high school [to start] later so we could sleep more. If middle and high school started later, then we would concentrate more because we would be more rested. . . . I would be more alert in class."

Ten-year-old Rashan wrote: "We also need . . . [to] sleep at night. We don't want to get sleepy at work or school. . . . You need lots of sleep and energy for the next day. If you can't go to sleep, try counting sheep that are jumping over your bed. Do you get a lot of sleep at night?"

Somehow, in the midst of our crammed schedules, we need to help our families get more rest. Try to let your children sleep in on a weekend day. Encourage them to go to bed earlier. When things get overwhelming, keep them home and let them catch up on their rest from time to time. With only twenty-four hours in a day, and ever more homework, activities, and scheduled events for our children, it can be a challenge. This is just one more reason to take a good hard look at all the demands on our children, and on us, and consider simplifying.

## SAFETY

Healthful living also means taking reasonable safety and security precautions. Don't assume your children can independently protect themselves—until you teach them to. It's a no-brainer to childproof your house—take care of plastic bags, poisonous cleansers, medications, electric sockets, alcohol, matches, and guns. Insist on car seats, seat belts, bike helmets. We all know it's important to create good habits early, and to model good habits yourself.

Once you have established a safe environment for your children, you should gradually cede responsibility for their safety to them. That kind of good judgment is one of the things they should be developing as they mature. It is also one of the things they struggle with, so you do have to stay involved, providing guidance up to and through adolescence. But notice—and praise—when your child decides for herself to cancel her plans because of a threatening snowstorm, or tunes up the brakes on his own bike, or puts away toys with small pieces before a much younger child comes to visit. Talk to your children—and practice—what to do when they are out riding scooters in the neighborhood on their own, or traveling by public bus with their friends, or if a stranger tries to strike up a conversation. This will help them feel in control of their own health and their own lives.

## CHILDREN CARE ABOUT THE HEALTH OF OTHERS

Many children wrote in about their own health problems and the health problems of loved ones:

> I would want a new heart for Grandpa.
> —Scott, 8

> What I really want that money can't buy is for cancer to go away. I loved my grandparents dearly, but I lost both of them to cancer. All

I would want a new heart for Grandpa Mathey. Scott

"I would want a new heart for Grandpa Mathey." Artist: Scott, age 8

the achievements I have gained I wanted them to see. I miss them and I want them back here on earth.

—Tim, 17

I want a cure for autism. . . . Two of my four younger brothers are autistic. . . . It makes me sad when I think about why my brothers are not able to talk or play normally like other children. I sometimes wonder if they know that I'm there and that I love them very much. I really hope that one day someone finds a cure.

—Alanna, 16

I am an asthmatic child. I was born with this problem. All my nine years I have felt different from other children. I can't play in gym as well as my other classmates. My dream is that I will be cured.

—Stephanie, 9

If I could have one thing that money can't buy, it would be good health. Ever since eighth grade, I have been struggling to stay healthy with my environmental allergies. I still, to this day, have not known a day to be symptom free. Whether it be a migraine headache, chronic fatigue, or even just a stuffy nose, I have some form of a symptom every day. . . . Just to feel what it is like to be completely healthy would be the one thing I want that money cannot buy.

—Bryan, 18

I want my Pop Pop to get well.

—Nicholas, 9

These children remind us of just how precious each day is. Of course, there are many health events that no amount of precaution can prevent. We can't deny that life can be painful. Bad things happen to good people. It is part of what it is to be human, and we can't

"My younger brother, Damian, is deaf in his left ear." Artist: Ricardo

entirely shelter our children from that reality, at least not indefinitely. When someone close to them is coping with serious health issues, perhaps the most important insight for kids is that there is a safety net, there is a web of support—and that they are part of it. In addition to involving them in the community of support for a loved one who is ill, help them express their own sadness, questions, and other emotions. When another child is sick, part of what your children can do is to welcome that child back into some form of normality, giving them a chance to play as usual, kid to kid, to the degree possible. As Christine, a fourth grader, put it: "I hope that all people that have a physical problem can be healed because its unfair for them to just sit and watch when someone plays something. They should be able to play too."

## HEALTH CARE FOR KIDS

I cannot avoid commenting on the state of affairs with family health care in the United States today. At last count, over forty million Americans had no health insurance whatsoever, typically because they can't afford it and/or their employment does not include health coverage. This is unacceptable, and sadly, too many children are suffering the consequences. According to a report by the Federal Interagency Forum on Child and Family Statistics issued in 2002, nearly 25 percent of children in the United States remain inadequately immunized, and most of these children are from low-income families without health insurance. The United States is the most prosperous nation on Earth with material wealth at the top that exceeds the great fortunes built in the gilded age of the railroad and oil barons. Federal military spending in our country exceeds the combined defense spending of all major industrial nations, and yet millions of American children have no place to go when they are sick. Better nutrition, more sleep, and saying no to drugs and alcohol won't help a little girl or boy who needs serious medical attention. Parents can't fix this national crisis, but we can speak up to our elected officials and demand affordable and accessible health care for all. It's something that kids really need and want that *only* money can buy.

## BALANCE

In the larger picture, health and well-being for adults and children are connected to slowing down and establishing a healthy pace of life. With stress-related diseases already epidemic—and on the rise—and

"My Grandmother to be alive." Artist: Lauren H., age 15

childhood depression and related ills increasing as well, we all need to decompress. Think balance. Look into things like yoga or aikido and explore other quiet practices that can be adopted early for lifelong health and equilibrium. Our hearts can be lightened and our bodies strengthened by a dose of simple living.

## FOR FURTHER READING

*Fast Food Nation: The Dark Side of the All-American Meal,* Eric Schlosser. New York, HarperCollins, 2002.

*Living with Childhood Cancer: A Practical Guide to Help Families Cope,* Leigh Woznick and Carol Goodheart. Washington, D.C., American Psychological Association, 2002.
  (A terrific resource book for parents and others coping with the heartache of childhood cancer or other serious illnesses.)

*What Are We Feeding Our Kids?* Michael Jacobson and Bruce Maxwell. New York, Workman Publishing Company, 1994.

*The Whole Parenting Guide: Strategies, Resources, and Inspiring Stories for Holistic Parenting and Family Living,* Alan Reder, Stephanie Renfrow Hamilton, and Phil Catalfo. New York, Broadway Books, 1999.

## ADDITIONAL RESOURCES

Child Life Council, 11820 Parklawn Drive, #202, Rockville, MD 20852, www.childlife.org
  (A nonprofit group offering publications on helping children cope with illness or pain.)

# Part Two

# Parenting Wisely in a Commercial World

# Chapter 11

————

# Shelter from the Storm

*If guys aren't athletic and handsome and if girls aren't thin and beautiful, like the ads on TV dictate, we soon begin to think we are without value.*

—Jason, 13

RAISING KIDS in today's consumer culture is difficult. Our children live in a virtual storm of television commercials, banner ads, billboards, logos, and product placements. How do we protect them and instill positive values and critical thinking? This chapter examines the forces that influence our kids' values and behavior, assesses the negative impact on our children, and then highlights strategies for parents who want to provide some shelter from the storm.

## A "MORE IS BETTER" CULTURE

Kids have been exposed to commercial messages for several generations now, but the intensity of overt marketing to children is new. We want our children to value the things in life that money can't buy, but there's a multibillion-dollar industry that wants them to spend their cash on everything from supersized candy bars to designer watches. Critics warn that advertising directed toward children may be contributing to the rising number of American children who are stressed out, depressed, hyperactive, obese, exhausted, insomniac, even violent. "Advertising is contributing greatly to a consumer identity in children in which they believe and behave as if they can't be happy unless they constantly acquire more goods and services," according to Allen Kanner, clinical psychologist at Wright Institute in Berkeley, California. Kids seem on the brink of losing so much that is precious: core values, family time, connection to community and nature, and creative down time. What many of them have instead is intense peer rivalry based on material goods.

As parents, we must become more aware of the forces influencing our children's values and behavior. Several factors contribute to our material culture (which Juliet Schor, author of *The Overspent American,* describes as the "see, want, borrow, buy" way of life), including the extraordinary affluence of the top segments of our society and a correlating national preoccupation with extravagant celebrity lifestyles. But the most insidious—and the clearest cause for distress—is marketing and advertising. The background noise in the United States today is the hum of ads sending us nonstop sales pitches, and our kids are especially vulnerable to their power.

## HOW BIG IS THE PROBLEM?

Marketers are openly courting children on an unprecedented scale, all in the name of creating brand loyalty as soon as a child is old enough to ask for a product by name, distinguish corporate logos, or recite product jingles. Usually, that's *not* old enough to go to school or even (reliably) to use the potty. Corporations go after children because lifetime customers add up to years of profitable revenue.

One advertising industry magazine (named *Kidscreen*—a whole journal devoted to selling to kids!) reports that ad agencies are now targeting "the 0–3 demographic." They call it "cradle-to-grave marketing." Kids are bombarded with ads all day long, at home, at school, and on the street. Their clothes (and their friends' clothes) are covered with commercial messages. Their time on the web is punctuated with ads. Add magazine, newspaper, radio, and of course television ads, along with movie product placements and commercial posters, and this is what you get: The average American child is exposed to *forty hours a week* of commercial messages, according to research from the Kaiser Family Foundation. The vast majority come from one source: television. Ninety-nine percent of children in the United States live in a home with one or more televisions. Nearly a third of all children live in homes with four or more TVs, and 24 percent of children under six have TVs in their bedrooms, according to data from 1996 in the *Journal of Advertising Research.*

Americans in general spend 40 percent of their free time watching television, and children are usually the most avid viewers, watching on average two and three-quarters hours on a typical day. The average twelve-year-old spends four hours a day watching TV. That's the same as two months per year of nonstop television!

The amount of time Americans—and kids in particular—spend in front of the tube has risen dramatically over recent decades. (Just as spending on advertising aimed at children has. Coincidence? You decide.) The average American child sees between twenty and forty *thousand* television commercials each year—more than fifty to a hundred every day.

Those who are concerned about the violence kids watch on TV are fighting the good fight. But the manipulative messages children see *between* programs are perpetrating another kind of violence directly on kids while they sit in front of the screen. The constant stream of commercial pitches to buy happiness warps children's spirits in its own devastating way.

By the time they are three, before they can read, many American kids are making specific requests for brand-name products. That's the payoff for years of sophisticated marketing to children: Experts have shown that at six months of age, as they are starting to make simple sounds like "ma-ma," babies are also beginning to form mental images of corporate logos and mascots. A 1991 study showed that 91 percent of six-year-olds could correctly identify Joe Camel with Camel cigarettes. Cigarettes! Teachers in preschools report that children know more television commercial jingles than traditional songs such as "Twinkle Twinkle Little Star" and the alphabet song. A friend of mine told me of her horror at attending her daughter's day care "spring show" only to hear the three-year-olds' rousing rendition of a song with this syncopated refrain: "McDonald's, McDonald's, Kentucky Fried Chicken, and a Pizza Hut!"

No wonder a Time/CNN poll showed that 71 percent of parents said their kids are exposed to too much advertising. Almost two out of three parents want networks to cut back on ads aimed at kids, and the same proportion say Internet providers are not doing enough to protect kids from online marketing. At best, kids who surf the web are being bombarded with ads in chat rooms and on Internet game and music sites. At worst, they are encouraged to buy pornographic or other destructive products. In a survey by National Public Radio, 31 percent of children ages ten to seventeen reported having seen a pornographic site on the Internet. According to a 1999 poll commissioned by the Center for a New American Dream, 87 percent of parents of children ages two to seventeen feel that advertising and marketing aimed at children make kids too materialistic, and a similar number say that these commercial forces are hurting kids' values.

## WHY HAS ADVERTISING TO KIDS SKYROCKETED?

Marketers follow the money, and many American children have cash to burn. Advertising to children has increased largely because the amount of money kids spend has risen dramatically. In 1991 kids spent $8.6 billion. In less than a decade, the figure was up to *$29 billion* spent out of allowances, baby-sitting and lawn-mowing money, holiday gifts, and parental handouts. The average preteen spends six hundred dollars a year—almost all of it on him- or herself.

Teenagers flex even more financial muscle. In 2001 teenagers spent roughly $172 billion of their own money, up from $63 billion just seven years earlier. Youth-oriented financial services encourage this trend with online spending accounts and prepaid credit cards for teens.

But that's not the end of the story. Children also influence their parents' spending to the tune of another $400 billion a year on groceries, restaurant meals, vacations, and even cars. That is, of course, only a partial list. Marketers call this influence "the nag factor" or "pester power." Children have gotten to be much more proficient naggers over the years—or their parents are more susceptible to their appeals. In the 1960s children ages four to twelve influenced about $5 billion worth of their parents' purchases. That increased tenfold by 1984 (to $50 billion) and more than tripled again by 1997 (to $188 billion), and still the rapid growth continues. By 2001 the number reached an estimated $300 billion.

So it's no wonder corporations shell out such enormous amounts of money for ads aimed directly at kids. Businesses spent a paltry $357 million on toy advertising in 1983, but bumped it up to $878 million by 1993. Marion Nestle, chair of the Department of Nutrition and Food Studies at New York University, estimates that $13 billion a year is spent marketing food and drinks to American children. The total dollars spent on marketing to kids is much higher when fashion branding; movie product placements; and direct ads via TV, radio, and teen magazines are combined.

Fortunately, parents can help protect kids from the influence of our commercial culture. The basic strategies are fairly straightforward: Limit exposure (especially television), teach your kids how advertising works so they won't be easily manipulated, offer positive alternatives to commercial entertainment, and join with others to restrict advertising to children.

## STRATEGIES FOR PROTECTING YOUR CHILDREN

*Limit your child's exposure to advertising.* The most obvious place to start is with television. Limit how much commercial TV your family watches. Start with having a set only in a common room—no televisions in your children's bedrooms. If your child already has a TV in the bedroom, he will undoubtedly howl about any change. Consider selling the bedroom television and letting him use the profits for something that will provide lasting pleasure: a guitar, basketball hoop, or, if both you and your child are willing to take on the responsibility, a pet. Decide how much TV is enough and agree on the rule for your family, be it an hour a day, two shows a week, or any other formula that feels right to you. Some parents take dramatic steps. Take David Dombeck in Nebraska: "Our first step against commercialism was to remove the TV from our home (done when our daughter was three). The past two years we have had a video monitor and VCR (which we use three or four times a month, at most) but we still do not have broadcast TV." Kim and Ken Burns from Kansas have a different approach: "Our family does not subscribe to any cable or satellite TV channels so we watch very little TV. For the six weeks of Lent we give up TV entirely. Instead of watching shows and even the local news at night, we play games, watch home movies, and rent movies from the library." Other parents take more modest approaches, setting limits on how much and what kind of commercial television can be viewed. As much as possible, offer constructive alternatives to TV programs and avoid using the television as an electronic baby-sitter.

Choose what you do watch carefully. Obviously, some television programming does have entertainment and educational value, but you have to weigh that against the dose of commercial messages bombarding your kids. In addition to limiting exposure to commercial television in the home, try to restrict exposure to highly commercial Internet providers, teen magazines, and nonstop commercial radio. Don't buy clothing adorned with corporate logos and avoid going to sections of stores that intentionally place candy or toys at eye level for an average six-year-old. You can't build a wall, but you can help guide your child toward noncommercial videos (or better yet, books) instead of TV; CDs or their own musical instrument instead of commercial radio; and magazines such as *Ladybug, Cricket,* or *New Moon* that forgo or restrict ads instead of *Your Magazine (YM)*, *Seventeen*, *Cosmo Girl*, or *Teen People*.

*Take a look at the influence of marketers in schools.* Kids spend most of their waking hours in one of two places: in front of the TV or in a classroom. So that's where advertisers make their heaviest pitches. The school-based cable news program Channel One (complete with commercials) is seen by more than eight million kids in about twelve thousand schools every day. Hundreds, if not thousands, of school districts across the country have deals with cola companies to promote their products—selling only a certain brand in their vending machines or plastering a corporate logo on the scoreboard. In 2000 *Advertising Age* reported that over just eighteen months, the number of these exclusive contracts increased 300 percent nationwide. The trend is still advancing. In one Colorado school district, administrators went even further and urged school principals to use new incentives to increase soda consumption because greater volumes sold would translate into more revenue for the school district. The irony is that most cola contracts actually generate relatively little income for schools.

If you hope to limit your child's exposure to commercial messages, you can't ignore your child's school. Visit the school and you may be surprised to find commercial posters and other ads in the hallways, cafeterias, gyms, and the classrooms themselves. School buses in some districts are plastered with corporate logos. Even some textbooks contain them. PTA and school fund-raisers increasingly involve partnerships that propel kids to sell corporate products. Even school discount booksellers such as Scholastic, supposedly promoting reading and a love of books, now also hawk noneducational products through schools, from commercial videos and toys to jewelry and electronic games.

You need to talk all this over with your child, but don't stop there. Ask the PTA to hold a meeting about commercialism in the school. Encourage the principal and teachers to get involved. Together you can analyze how and when commercial messages are reaching children and how to limit the influence of corporations in schools. You may be able to band together with like-minded adults to get the school to reconsider its involvement with Channel One, its sale of junk food during lunch, and its corporate-related fund-raising efforts involving children. Consider having your school participate in TV-Turn-Off Week.

No public institution should become just another billboard for yet another commercial message. Our kids have a right to expect some shelter in their schools, as well as in their homes.

*Teach your children the ABCs of advertising.* Don't simply reduce exposure; help your children analyze advertising. Watch commercial TV together and point out how ads attempt to sell popularity, fun, and success—any number of specific kinds of happiness. Encourage your kids to decode the ads for you. You can make it into a thinking game: "What are the advertisers selling and how?" Kathy Sessions, a mother in Maryland, wrote in with the following story: "Our five-year-old was recently in the grocery store with her father, spotted a prominent display of candy and toys near the checkout counter, and exclaimed, 'There's a trick for children!' because her father had, on a previous trip, explained how stores often put candy and toys at children's eye level or out front to try to get the kids to pester their parents to buy them. A very basic explanation helped give her a bit of immunity from the automatic 'gimmes.'" Help your kids understand the companies' marketing techniques. Children as young as four or five can develop this critical media literacy.

Most ads suggest that kids will find friends, love, group acceptance, fun, and respect by purchasing particular products, and those aimed at children hit particularly hard on fitting in. You might see how your kids react to the following interpretation of advertising to kids, described by Nancy Shalek, former president of Grey Advertising, as reported in the *Los Angeles Times*: "Advertising at its best is making people feel that without their product, you're a loser. Kids are very sensitive to that. If you tell them to buy something, they are resistant. But if you tell them they'll be a dork if they don't, you've got their attention." Kids don't like being manipulated any more than you do, so the ad spell is easy to break once you show them how it works.

It is never too early to alert your children to the seduction techniques of advertising. As they get older, you and your children can analyze ads in more sophisticated ways. How are the advertisers using music? How are they using color? What emotions are they evoking? How are they trying to make you feel? Why? One or two months of regular deconstruction of ads should be sufficient. Ask your child if she really thinks eating a particular brand of potato chips will make her popular or if a certain toy will win her new and lasting friends, as the ads suggest. If you carry on with this strategy too long or with tedious repetition, it might backfire and your kids may tune *you* out. In most cases, this short-term analytic approach to commercials gives your kids a sort of vaccination, one that will keep working even as they enter adolescence. Once "vaccinated," their first response to any ad will not be "I want it" (advertisers' desired effect), but rather "What are they selling, and how?" (parents' desired effect).

Even if the "I want it" comes later, which of course it sometimes does, you are ahead of the game. You've created a distance from sales pitch to desire—a little breathing room for rational decision-making. This is essentially a way to empower your children and to help them think critically about billboards, radio ads, logos, and the general culture. It's home-based media literacy training, and I can't overemphasize its importance.

## OFFER POSITIVE ALTERNATIVES TO COMMERCIALISM

Encourage creative alternatives to commercial TV watching and web surfing. Whenever we say no to some things, it's often helpful to say yes to something more positive. That can mean suffering through messy arts and crafts or noisy banging of drums—but it's a great trade-off in the long run. Help your children get together with friends, play outside, and explore new interests. Let them get bored and fidget without resorting to the immediate TV or video game "fix." Most creative play and work emerges from unstructured time. Help your child grow more self-reliant and resourceful by *not* resorting to commercial entertainment too often. The next chapter will give you lots of specific suggestions for helping your children have more fun with less stuff.

## TEACH YOUR CHILDREN TO BE WARY OF THE "BUY NOW, PAY LATER" CULTURE

Once your kids are on to the marketers and advertisers, you are well on your way to equipping them to be careful consumers. We live in a commercial world, and our children will be well served if we teach them to be wary of the incessant offers of credit and layaway plans. Kids need early education about money, savings, and how to buy wisely.

*Consider the importance of delayed gratification.* Many kids and adults seem hell-bent on fulfilling all their material aspirations immediately, and dozens of lending institutions make it easy to buy now and pay later. Sadly, this risky approach to spending has forced millions of families into financial jeopardy. Young people are especially vulnerable to the nonstop offers of free credit cards and instant happiness. Through the 1990s, college students' average credit card debt jumped 250 percent, from $900 to $2,250. Because credit card debt includes a steep interest rate, it's all too easy to lose financial control. College administrators report that student financial mismanagement is a huge and growing problem.

*Focus on savings.* Parents can help kids prepare for these seductive offers of instant pleasure in several ways. First, when you think the time is right, talk about credit cards and the dangers of buying with interest payments. Then, make sure your children have their own bank accounts and suggest regular deposits out of their allowance or any other money they earn or receive as gifts. Reinforce the value of

saving with lots of praise, and talk about your own savings and investment plans so your children feel part of the family's financial planning. Whether you hide cash under your mattress or invest in mutual
funds, let your children know that setting money aside for future
needs and dreams is extremely important.

*Talk about the dangers of gambling.* The "get rich quick" gambling syndrome is rampant in our society. What once was morally
frowned upon and outright banned is now ubiquitous. Numerous
states operate and promote lotteries, and weekend gambling trips are
popular vacation getaways. Children need to learn early about the
dangers of gambling and the potential for financial losses. Helping
kids to be responsible stewards of money can give them a lifelong
financial life jacket.

## TEACH YOUR CHILDREN TO BE
## RESPONSIBLE CONSUMERS

There is more to responsible consuming than just wise money management. Help your kids think before they spend, both about whether
they really want or need a particular new product and about what
questions to ask when making a purchase. I've already indicated that
the best antidote to the insatiable desire for more stuff is daily living
focused on meeting authentic nonmaterial desires. But as part of this
whole exercise, you may need to get a grip on shopping. Don't laugh:
Shopping is the number two form of recreation in this country, right
after television. We have 24,000 high schools in this country—and
42,130 shopping centers. Eighty-eight percent of teenage girls say
they just "love to shop."

Shopping does provide novelty and social interaction, as well as
the thrill of the hunt—legitimate human needs—which are all part of
why we like doing it. I sometimes enjoy shopping with my daughter
now that she's hit her teen years (although I often wish there were
better product choices for adolescent girls). But shopping is not a

sport. Try to avoid impulse shopping as a coping strategy for depression or loneliness. Too many of us simply shop to fill some need . . . so we shop for nothing in particular. Only 25 percent of mall shoppers surveyed across the country were there for a particular item.

When your kids plan to make a purchase, teach them to be critical thinkers. Americans have always been adept at assessing things such as price and quality. But the times cry out for us to ask some new questions when we go to the cash register. Encourage your children to pause and think about where things come from, who makes them, and where the products eventually go when they're tossed in the trash. This is complex enough for adults, so try to keep your analysis simple. Take paper. It comes from trees—too often from ancient old-growth forests or clear-cut lands that we want to protect, but sometimes paper (paper towels, toilet paper, copier paper, note cards, napkins, and more) comes from forests that are managed carefully for the long haul. Let your kids know that you want to buy paper from responsible companies that are trying to take care of the land. You can involve them in buying recycled paper products in order to conserve trees. Seek out these alternative products and involve your kids in this whole new approach to consuming. It's got to be part of what we teach them (and ourselves) for the coming decades.

Help your kids understand how our new global economy works; and how behind every product is a faraway story of someone who made and assembled the soccer ball, the tennis shoe, or the T-shirt. Read the label and most likely you'll see that the product was made in China, Taiwan, Vietnam, Indonesia, Nepal, or Mexico. Most things are now made overseas and merely designed, marketed, and disposed of in the United States.

You can't scrutinize every single purchase, but when the information is available, try to determine whether products are made under humane working conditions and in environmentally friendly ways. The two big questions all consumers need to start asking are, Is this product coming from a factory where people are treated and paid fairly? and Is this product made and packaged to protect the natural environment? In most cases, we don't know. But environmental, labor, and consumer groups are working hard to get this information to the public, so keep your eyes open for new consumer labels and information. You can get your child started with a few easy purchases: an organic cotton T-shirt (that greatly reduces pesticide use and chemical exposure for farm workers), a compact disc packaged only in recycled cardboard (not plastic), 100 percent recycled printer paper for the home computer, locally grown fruit and vegetables, an energy-efficient computer, or nontoxic cosmetics made without animal testing. Instill the lifelong search for environmentally and worker-friendly products. As with analyzing advertising, you have to be careful not to turn into a total bore on the subject, while still giving kids the tools they need to evaluate their purchases.

## HOW MUCH IS ENOUGH?

In the end, we need to help our kids regularly consider if they really want or need any given item—and why. Perhaps the most fundamental question to instill in your kids is this one: How much is enough? Talk about it with them. In a world where two billion people live on one dollar a day or less, how many plastic toys do your children really need? In a world where Americans already consume nearly 30 percent of the world's material resources, do we need more? This is a reality many of us would prefer to ignore, but we can't. Obviously, not all American families are affluent, but many are, on a global scale. You may have your own way of addressing these issues without being too heavy-handed, but consider examining these core issues of equity and environmental impact. It's vital that we help our children understand American materialism in a global context. If the world becomes completely divided into groups of haves versus have-nots, who can be truly content? If our consumerism causes unintentional but irreversible environmental or human damage, who can feel safe? This deep understanding of our oneness, our interconnected world, is a key part of what children need to grasp as they grow up in such a commercial world.

## HELP CHANGE THE SYSTEM

In the best of all worlds, our elected leaders would require corporations to limit advertising to children. Sweden and the Canadian province of Quebec forbid advertising to children under twelve. Most European countries place some form of restriction on marketing to children. There are growing signs of discontent in the United States as well, with many school districts banning commercial vending machines and commercial television in schools. Still, an outright ban or restriction on advertising to children in the United States is almost unimaginable in our current political climate. The federal Government Accounting Office—the research arm of Congress—released a study in September 2000 showing the rising influence of corporations in public schools, but no federal action was taken. Free enterprise, for all its positive side, needs to operate within certain limits, yet apparently, when it comes to our kids, there are none. Companies are free to market almost anything to anybody anywhere—regardless of the impact on our children. A survey released by the U.S. Federal Trade Commission in June 2002 found that children are frequently exposed to ads for online gambling on nongambling web sites despite laws requiring businesses to issue warnings about underage gambling prohibitions. This "anything goes" value system is deeply ingrained in our national fabric despite growing parental protests. For inspiration we should look to the successful bans on cigarette advertising to children and keep pushing for more comprehensive policies that protect our kids, especially very young children, from commercial messages. Talk to your elected officials, write to the most egregious companies, and join national campaigns aimed at limiting advertising to children.

## BE A POSITIVE ROLE MODEL AND TEAM UP

As with so much else, children learn from what we do as well as what we say. Consider this yet another chance to examine things such as your television viewing habits, spending and credit card practices, consumer choices, and more. Remember that none of us are perfect— not even close. So don't go this road alone. Find others who want to join you in this journey and bring your families together. It is often helpful to kids to know they aren't the only ones living with limited TV and video games, or not hanging out at the mall every weekend, or wearing what's comfortable rather than what's "in."

If you are feeling alone in this uphill struggle, or if you're look- ing for a more organized approach, you might start or join a support group, gathering with other parents who share your concerns, meet- ing once a month to swap strategies for healthy child-raising, and soliciting advice on your own sticky situations. You could organize one or more PTA meetings on these issues, with a focus on the com- mercialization of schools. You really *can* make a difference: In 2001, for example, the Madison, Wisconsin, school board ended its rela- tionship with the Coca Cola company after immense public outcry. According to an Associated Press article in May 2002, Maine, New York, New Jersey, Maryland, Colorado, Nebraska, and Idaho estab- lished, due to parental demands, statewide restrictions on the sale of junk food in schools. The Center for a New American Dream has information for parents on how to examine commercialism in schools. Check out our web site at www.newdream.org or write to Kids and Commercialism Program, Center for a New American Dream, 6930 Carroll Avenue, Suite 900, Takoma Park, Maryland 20912.

But what if your kids still nag? Talk to them. Don't just say no. That no can sometimes seem like a dogmatic and undemocratic prohi- bition to a child. Your children may suggest that you are terminally unhip and that you don't understand the importance of whatever item is currently hotly sought. What you can do in return is speak honestly about your values, concerns, and precisely why you will not purchase a particular item—because it's too sexually provocative, violent, plas- tic, dumb, expensive, or just totally unnecessary and based on hard- core marketing, not genuine wants and needs. If you follow these basic rules, your children will be more likely to adopt your values over time:

- Limit their exposure to commercial messages, primarily by limiting commercial television.
- Equip them to analyze ads so they can't be so easily manipulated.

"... for people all over the world to treat each other with love and respect."
Artist: Makayla, age 7

- Offer them positive alternatives to commercial entertainment and shopping as an antidote to boredom or low self-esteem.
- Remain consistent with your household rules and communicate your values.
- Walk the talk as best you can.
- Periodically buy some things that *will* provide true entertainment, growth, or lasting pleasure.
- Embrace the things kids say they really want that money can't buy, and you'll discover that their nagging diminishes in proportion to the happiness they are finding in other places.

When the going gets rough or you feel it's all hopeless, just remember that in the long run your kids will deeply appreciate your efforts to protect them from commercialism. Nobody has all the answers, so we can only do our best. When you say no and teach them other ways, you are expressing your own powerful need to protect, nurture, and support the best in your children. And that is exactly what they really want that money can't buy, even if they can't always see it in the midst of pestering you!

## FOR FURTHER READING

*Affluenza: The All-Consuming Epidemic,* John DeGraaf, David Wann, and Thomas Naylor. San Francisco, Berret-Koehler Publishers, 2001.
(A lively overview of consumer culture in the United States.)
*The Age of Missing Information,* Bill McKibben. New York, Random House, 1992.
(A fascinating personal account about the contrasting realities of media-driven daily life and the rhythms of the natural world.)
*Deadly Persuasion: Why Women and Girls Must Fight the Addictive Power of Advertising,* Jean Kilbourne. New York, The Free Press, 1999.
(An important critique of the impact of commercialism on girls.)
*Commodify Your Dissent: The Business of Culture in the New Gilded Age,* Thomas Frank and Matt Weiland. New York, W.W. Norton, 1997.
(A biting collection of essays about commercial culture and its impact on American values and lifestyles.)

*Creating Ever-Cool: A Marketer's Guide to a Kid's Heart,* Gene Del Vecchio.
Gretna, LA, Pelican Publishing Co., 1998.
(An inside perspective on marketing strategies for controlling and manipulating children's desires.)

## ADDITIONAL RESOURCES

*Tips for Parenting in a Commercial Culture,* a pamphlet with helpful tips available from the Center for a New American Dream, 6930 Carroll Avenue, Suite 900, Takoma Park, Maryland 20912, www.newdream.org
*The Cost of Cool,* www.videoproject.net/cost_of_cool_exp.htm
(A riveting video that exposes the harmful impacts of advertising on teen culture, produced by Population Communications International.)
The Henry J. Kaiser Family Foundation, www.kff.org
(This web site has extensive research data on the impact of media and technology on children.)
Consumers Union, www.zillionsedcenter.org
(This web site for kids helps children become responsible consumers.)
Commercial Alert, 3719 SE Hawthorne Blvd., #281, Portland, OR 97214, www.commercialalert.org
(A national advocacy group working to limit advertising to children.)

# Chapter 12

―――――――――

# More Fun, Less Stuff

*If you never did, you should.*
*These things are fun and fun is good!*
　　　　　　　　　　　　　　—Dr. Seuss

PERHAPS THE MOST ENJOYABLE WAY to snap your kids out of shopaholic inclinations is to refocus them on noncommercial ways to enjoy themselves. If they are having a good time, they won't need or want to concentrate on material ways to make themselves feel good. In a nutshell: more fun, less stuff.

Many parents feel nostalgic for the childhoods they experienced—a slower pace in an era when kids could be kids and families were more tightly knit. We wish our own kids could have more opportunities to simply play, explore, develop friendships, and have fun away from malls, televisions, and scheduled activities. They deserve memories about more than work, spending, and racing to the next activity.

But today the activities that could bring deeper meaning and enjoyment to kids' daily lives are often squeezed out. This is the first generation to be raised with a rattle in one hand and a mouse in the other. So many pastimes that have entertained adults and kids alike for millennia—storytelling, singing, games, outdoor adventure, dancing—have ceded to electronic entertainment or highly organized activities. We rent videos, listen to CDs, watch dancers on MTV. We find our fun through observing rather than doing. This is reflected in a cartoon my daughter recently cut out of the newspaper for me showing a kid glued to the TV—watching another kid fly a kite.

It's more than a little ironic that the vast majority of ads and commercials directed at children are designed to sell them something—chips, shoes, toys—using images of kids outdoors, kids dancing, kids doing precisely what kids should be doing, but . . . our kids aren't doing those things. They're watching the actors in the ads doing them. Our kids watch and often conclude that if they buy whatever is being pitched, they will be transformed into those happy, hip, fun-loving kids on the screen. It is a bizarre, and sad, reality.

Electronic forms of entertainment are fun—they're just dominating our lives too much relative to other possibilities. So the trick is to find some balance and hold on to old-fashioned play because it is active, and interactive. Beyond the plain old fun of them, these kinds of activities connect us one to another, something both kids and parents say they really want.

Many adults—and many kids too—have forgotten how to just play. Play isn't goal oriented; it exists for its own sake. Old-fashioned fun is regenerative; a dose of it is a mood-elevator. Of course we have to free up the time for it to happen, which means setting limits on how much time our kids spend in structured activities or in front of television. It's noteworthy that 83 percent of teachers—according to one national survey—feel that parents fail to control how much time their kids spend with TV, computers, and video games and believe it's a serious problem.

The Center for a New American Dream's motto is, More fun, less stuff, and we've become pros at collecting other people's suggestions on how to have fun without spending a dime. I hope these suggestions will rekindle fond childhood memories or introduce you to some new ideas. There are plenty of recommendations here to get

I would like to go on a surf trip.

"I would like to go on a surf trip." Artist: Chadd

your juices flowing, but often the key to fun is just giving kids some free time alone or with other kids, away from other distractions.

Be prepared to handle a certain amount of whining when your kids' electronic standbys are ruled out. Stand firm and know in your heart that you are actually meeting your children's true needs, and even their real desires. There will inevitably be the youthful "Oh Mom" (or "Oh Dad"). "That's so boring" or "That's so stupid" eye-rolling reactions to various proposals, yet try to persevere. Today no self-respecting ten-year-old wants to see a G-rated movie, and likewise, the thought of painting, building a playhouse, or camping may be greeted with something less than enthusiasm. Plunge ahead anyway. Typically, once they get over the initial hurdle of resistance, kids do get turned on by what really makes them feel alive and happy. It can start as cultural combat, but it usually ends with laughter. Really. And like so many things, the more you do it, the easier and more natural it becomes.

But remember, you don't have to be your children's camp director (which they'd probably resent anyway). You don't need to be forever orchestrating the perfect fun experience. Not every plan needs to be an elaborate one. For the most part, let your kids come up with what they want to do, even if initially they aren't sure how to do it. Great ideas emerge from a little boredom or frustration.

Oh, and be prepared to tolerate a mess. If your children aren't sitting still in one place (in front of a TV or computer or video game), they might transform their surroundings, and this is what you want; messy is a natural state of affairs when you are sculpting, cooking, gardening, or building a fort with every last pillow in the house. They might track in dirt after a group hike in the woods, or get sawdust all over the basement floor when they make a birdhouse, or accidentally get a certain amount of glue in their hair while working on a collage. Put down newspapers. Learn to live with it. Think of it as part of the play in progress. (And get your kids to take the lead on handling the cleanup!)

I'll admit that a lot of this is easier for younger kids. As your children hit the teen years, it gets to be more of a challenge. We've heard some protests in our house—when you're going after something so low tech, you're definitely at risk of kids thinking it is "dumb." You may have to shift your strategy or refine your approach—or rely more on your kids to set a tone you both agree to—but don't give up. This is not an impossible dream. You're never too old to have fun.

## IDEAS TO GET YOU STARTED

To get you started, I've compiled a list of practical, creative ideas for having old-fashioned fun—maximizing play while minimizing stuff. Many don't cost a penny, and most are low cost. Some things do cost money (although they certainly don't have to be expensive), but they don't involve accumulating unnecessary stuff and they do have value above and beyond the monetary (the way travel does, or going to arts performances).

I've divided the list into several categories to help you zero in on what your children are interested in. Many will be familiar to you. Watch for something new that might resonate with your own children. What makes them laugh? What makes them lighthearted? Do more of that! For that matter, what makes you laugh? What makes you lighthearted? Do more of that too, and include your family. Think back to your fondest childhood memories, and see which are possible to recreate for your kids.

## Baking and Cooking

- Bake bread. Knead it, let it rise, pound it down.
- Harvest some fruit or vegetables from a local "pick your own" farm. Join with other families either to pick or even can or freeze what you've gathered.
- Pull out a favorite cookie recipe and indulge your sweet tooth; perhaps even make enough to share with a neighbor, or with your child's class, or to send off in a care package to someone you love.
- Teach your child how to make his or her favorite meal.
- Have your teenager organize a "bake-off" with friends and swap baked goods while hanging out together.
- Encourage your children to create and run a restaurant in your own home for one night every now and then, complete with menus, wait staff, candles, and so on.

## Words

- Tell stories. Be funny, scary, inspiring, bizarre. Fact or fiction, you choose. Make them up as you go along, or retell stories from books. Take turns developing a narrative together. Recall

"Friends, Fun, Good times." Artist: Christine, age 16

family stories or tales of when your children were younger.

- Read—together or each on your own. It is relaxing, pleasurable, and a great way to unwind. Start a family book club.
- Write a letter to a friend or relative.
- Visit the library and check out a bunch of books. Sometimes kids who resist reading may respond to collections of short stories, magazines, or comics.

- Help your kids start a youth newsletter reporting on the family, the neighborhood, or school.
- Keep journals, individually and/or as a family.
- Enjoy crossword puzzles or other word games.

## Games

- Teach your children your favorite games from your childhood, classics like kick the can, capture the flag, charades, hopscotch, tag, or hide-and-seek. Learn a game from your kids or learn a new one together. Invent new games, or modify old ones.
- Play board games. Even teenagers love them. Yes, this may require buying a game (Boggle, Taboo, Balderdash, Scrabble, Chess, Cranium, and Clue are some favorites), but a well-loved and well-worn game is a worthwhile investment.
- Play group problem-solving games, such as math games, or hold a mystery "whodunit?" dinner party for your teenager.
- Play cards. A pack of cards is inexpensive, portable, and useful in a large variety of ways. Besides games, learn some card tricks, or build card houses.
- Pay catch! Now here's an all-American pastime you can play just about anywhere that you can find a little outdoor space. You get to be outside and use your body a bit. You can have a leisurely talk with your catching partner without the pressure of face-to-face conversation. You'll most likely cross paths with your neighbors. You'll get better with practice. For variety, try kicking a ball back and forth.
- Play outdoor games. Have fun and get some fresh air at the same time. Drag out the badminton, croquet, or volleyball set gathering dust in the basement. Ultimate Frisbee is a winner with older kids. Or play horseshoes—even if it means just planting a stick in the ground and pitching rocks at it.
- Play silly games. These are great at a party, but you can do

them anytime you've got a good-size group. Pass a grapefruit held between the chin and neck (hands behind your back), do a relay race with an egg on a spoon, roll basketballs with your noses to the finish line.

- Create a treasure hunt. Hide something either inside or outside your house and hand out clues to lead your kids there. You can make visual clues for kids who don't read yet. Or try a scavenger hunt.

## Drama

- Put on a play. If you have a video camera, film it. Your children will love to watch that tape even years later.
- Again, if you have or can borrow a video camera, let your older kids make their own movie. Or put together a special video for distant friends or relatives to bring them up-to-date on the family.
- Organize a neighborhood or family talent show.
- Put on a puppet show. (You could even make some or all of the puppets yourself!)

## Natural Fun

- Take a walk in the woods. Invite other families to join you on a hiking trail. Bring along a Frisbee or football.
- Go bird watching. Learn the names of the local birds, and keep an eye out for rarer sightings. Make a bird feeder. Build your own, or simply spread peanut butter and birdseed on a pinecone to hang from a tree.
- Stargaze. Go to the library for a basic book about the constellations, then head out one night to a dark open space to lie on blankets or in sleeping bags and look up at the stars. Or visit a planetarium. Many communities have organized events around meteor showers and other sky spectacles, and you may find amateur astronomers who will let you look through their

telescopes at craters on the moon or the rings of Saturn. Contact your local natural history museum, planetarium, or observatory for information. Check out *Discover the Stars* by Richard Berry, or *Stargazing for Beginners* by John Mosley. Or go to www.skyandtelescope.com where you can print out sky charts for your neighborhood and get some hints on star watching, including for beginners.

- Fly a kite.
- Make a homemade fishing pole; attach a string and simple hook from your local hardware store, and go to a pond or river in search of a fish.
- Camp. This could mean sleeping bags in your own back-yard—or honing survival skills in the wilderness. Try it; you might like it.
- Grow something. Plant a small garden, or flower bed, or a window box, or house plants. Kids especially love to grow something they can eat. Start from seeds or seedlings or cut-tings. Even just sprouting some seeds can feel like your own personal miracle. Brighten up winter by forcing bulbs inside. Try paper whites, hyacinth, or amaryllis. See *Forcing, Etc.* by Katherine Whiteside, *Flowering Bulbs for Dummies* by Judy Glattstein, or another book at your local library for specific directions. Or go to www.gardenersnet.com/hplants/hp6.htm.
- Pick a wildflower bouquet.
- Make homemade skateboard or scooter ramps and jumps. Ask your town for a safe place to have a skate park.
- Have a tea party or picnic.
- Go cloud watching. Bring friends and family and share with one another the different shapes you see in the sky.
- Create a backyard wildlife sanctuary, a welcoming habitat for native animals and plants. Plant flowers and fruiting plants that attract birds and butterflies, build animal feeders and shelters, provide plenty of greenery for shelter. Plant species indigenous to your area, which will mean that they won't require fertilizers, pesticides, or extra water once they are

established. Even in an apartment, a window box of purple bee balm can entice butterflies, or a bird feeder can draw birds. Or adopt a neglected area of public space nearby, clean out any litter, then scatter birdseed so all the neighbors can enjoy a little wildlife. Make your sanctuary where you can easily keep an eye on it, from the kitchen or out the living room window. Visit the library to learn how indigenous creatures like to live and how to tempt them to your house. Or contact the National Wildlife Federation's Backyard Habitat Program (8925 Leesburg Pike, Vienna, VA 22184-0001 or www.nwf.org/habitats) for specific directions. The *Wild Ones Handbook* on native species and landscaping for wildlife may also be useful: www.epa.gov/glnpo/greenacres/wildones /#HANDBOOK.

- Press flowers or leaves. Collect samples on a hike, or a walk through your neighborhood or just your own yard. Place your samples between sheets of absorbent paper under a heavy book until dry.

- "Vermicompost." That is, use worms to compost food and plant materials. It doesn't stink or take a lot of maintenance; plus you and your kids get to play with dirt and worms! And it is good for the environment—including your own immediate environment since it provides excellent nutrition for your garden. For how-to details on creating your own red wiggler worm bin, see *Worms Eat My Garbage: How to Set Up and Maintain a Worm Composting System* by Mary Appelhof, or the author's web site at www.wormwoman.com. Another good resource is www.wormdigest.org.

## Arts and Crafts

- Draw. Fill a sketchbook. Use various media, whatever stimulates your creativity. Draw outdoors with sidewalk chalk.
- Create scrapbooks. You can work chronologically, of course,

or pick a specific theme to organize around, such as a hobby, a vacation, or a holiday.

- Make a collage. Old magazines are always a good source for images, but don't limit yourself. Play with textures. Work with yarn, fabric, flowers and leaves, buttons and paperclips and beads—anything. Teenagers often love to build collages of pictures, personal souvenirs, concert ticket stubs, and photos of friends as a way to express their identities and personal passions.

- Make something with wood. Be your own carpenter, or carve or turn or whittle. One way or the other, create something beautiful and durable and perhaps useful. If you don't already have them around the house, you may need to buy tools, but a small investment will get you the basic penknife, saw, sandpaper, and chisel. Or borrow from a friend or neighbor. Start small. Make cooking spoons, a key chain, a footstool, a CD storage unit, or a set of blocks. Or just art! Either way, look for the natural beauty in the wood. See www.forestworld.com for information about wood, or www.taunton.com/finewoodworking/index.asp or www.sculptor.org/Wood for information on supplies and woodworking clubs. Ask for the Forest Stewardship Council (FSC) label when buying wood from Home Depot, Lowes, or other hardware stores to be sure you're buying wood that has been harvested responsibly. Wood is an environmental product we all can ask for! Not only is creating something with your own hands truly rewarding, but it also gives you a new sense of appreciation for artisans' skills and efforts and a fresh perspective on the true worth of an object.

- Knit, crochet, quilt, or sew—and don't make the mistake of thinking this is for girls only. You might approach an older relative or neighbor to offer a few introductory lessons to three or five children who would enjoy learning together.

- Paint. Experiment with different media: finger paints, watercolors, washable paints. Paint flower pots, or picture frames, or a cardboard box race car/playhouse/treasure chest. Use face or body paint to make your own "temporary tattoo" or disguise. Cover a whole wall with paper and make a mural. Or paint a room, or a piece of sculpture.

- Play with clay. Make homemade play dough. Learn to throw clay on a pottery wheel. Bend wire into forms. Use garden trimmings and yard waste to create outdoor sculptures. Glue "found objects" together into entirely new forms.
- Try printing with stamps made out of rubber erasers, potatoes, apples, sponges, or anything else you can devise. Test the limits of what you can make with thumb and finger prints.
- Make a book. Create doll clothes—or dolls, for that matter. Put together a personalized family calendar. Design your own clothes, or put together creative outfits or costumes at thrift or consignment shops. Keep and decorate a scrapbook.

## Movement

- Get in the water: Swim, run through the sprinkler, hike *in* a shallow stream, jump the waves, stomp in puddles. Or get on the water: Rent a canoe for the afternoon (it can be very inexpensive at some national parks) or some other boat (always with life preservers, of course).
- Skate—on ice or concrete, on in-line skates or roller skates or ice skates. Ride a scooter or skateboard.
- Jump rope. Skip. Use a hula hoop. Climb the monkey bars. Learn to walk on stilts, or work a pogo stick. Juggle.
- Make an obstacle course in your backyard, or in your house on a rainy or cold day. Or create your own ropes course.
- Do a home yoga program. Learn some basic poses, teach your kids, then let them teach their friends. It's a great and fun antidote to heavy backpacks and upper back problems caused by excess time on the computer, and stress of all kinds.
- Ride bikes. Ride together as a family, and teach your children

to ride safely on their own so they'll have their own personal form of reliable transportation. Try daylong trips.

- Play sports. Get friends and neighbors together for a pickup softball or volleyball game. No matter what their age or skill level, organize adults' and children's games of football, Wiffle ball, basketball, baseball, or soccer.
- Dance. You'll get exercise, stress-release, social interaction, exposure to cultural traditions, and fun all in one. Push the living room or bedroom furniture aside and boogie to your favorite CD in the privacy of your own home. Check out an instructional video from the library, and invite friends to come over and give it a whirl with you. Take lessons, or find a group that meets regularly with a mechanism in place for welcoming newcomers. Try moving to salsa or swing, African rhythms, a Viennese waltz, or the hustle and stomp and kick of an Irish beat. Step dance is popular with many teens. There are plenty of programs for beginners, so don't let inexperience stand in your way. Check the yellow pages or bulletin boards in coffee houses, bookshops, and music stores for groups and dances.

## Music

- Play an instrument. Go back to an old favorite, set aside time for a neglected love, or take lessons to learn to play. Play for yourself, play for your family, play for friends. Let your kids make noise!
- Improvise. Get a few friends together and use buckets, sticks, spoons, pots and pans, and whatever else inspires you to create a rhythm band . . . no expertise necessary.
- Sing. Sing in the shower or alone in your car. Turn up the radio or put on a favorite album and sing right along—like you mean it. Join a choir. Look for an accompanist if you are so inclined. A fourth grader on a recorder might do. Start a song circle—just gather enthusiastic singers, put together song sheets or a songbook, take turns choosing songs, and then just

sing. Pick a time, date, and location (your home? a community center?) and announce it to friends, advertise it in a community newspaper or neighborhood newsletter, or post fliers. Invite people to bring instruments, or sing a cappella. However and whenever you sing, don't worry about how it sounds, just enjoy! For inspiration, consult *Rise Up Singing: The Group Singing Songbook* by Peter Blood and Annie Patterson; *Songs and Creations* by Yohann Anderson; *For the Beauty of the Earth* by Pete Seeger, Raffi, John Denver, Tom Paxton, Tom Lehrer, Bill Staines, and John Gorka; or *Sing for Freedom: The Story of the Civil Rights Movement through Its Songs* edited by Guy and Candie Carawan.

- Make your own instruments. Seal the ends of a cardboard tube with rice inside, or sandwich dry beans between two paper plates. Turn empty oatmeal canisters into drums. "Play" a comb. String different size rubber bands around a shoe box.

## Scary Stuff

- Kids love to be scared—but not really. This is the faux terror that makes roller coasters such fun. But you can evoke the same thrills closer to home. Start with ghost stories on a stormy night, or in front of the fireplace with the lights out.
- Make a haunted house. Don't wait for Halloween. Provide visuals via video or makeup or cleverly chosen props. Don't forget a spooky soundtrack and costumes.

## Make Believe

- Fill a huge box with dress-up clothes, starting with your hand-me-downs and replenished with thrift store finds.
- Build a clubhouse for fantasy play using cardboard boxes, ropes, packing materials—whatever you can liberate from your attic or basement. Or for older kids—if you have the

space—let them build a more permanent structure from scrap wood, or perhaps take over a corner of the basement as their own, made private, perhaps with curtains created from old sheets hanging from the ceiling, and decorated inside to their liking.

- Make up stories to tell each other in the course of other activities. On a walk in the nearby woods, pretend to be on safari. Bring binoculars. Watch out for tigers. Make a trip to the grocery store a treasure hunt. Don't get too close to the alligator in aisle five, and watch out for the quicksand near the bakery counter. Spin a tale together about where the truck in front of you in traffic has been and where it is going.

## Toys

- All kids like novelty—their friends' toys are inherently more fascinating than their own. It's normal to get bored with the contents of one's same old toy chest. But does that always have to mean a trip to the store? Kids can look to each other instead. In my neighborhood there's a Toy Trade each year outside the local library, and families set up card tables outside to barter and exchange the stuff kids have grown out of or tired of. If there's nothing like it near you, think about establishing one with your kids, for the neighborhood, the school, your block, or, depending on the size of your extended family, the cousins.
- Yard sales are a great source for new (to your kids) toys. Consider having one yourself when the closet full of now unwanted, unused stuff really starts to overflow.
- Make toys. This is both an art project and a source of new playthings.
- Look for (or organize) a toy lending library. Many libraries, community colleges, and recreation centers sponsor them. Most were originally designed with child care providers in mind, but now usually anyone can sign up to check out toys.

## Building Community

- Have fun and get to know your neighbors at the same time. Attend community-organized dances or sports leagues. Organize a block party. Plan neighborhood potlucks or progressive dinners (appetizers at one house, entrées down the block, dessert and coffee at another home). Join your neighborhood association or the PTA, and be its social chair, if there isn't one already. On occasion, just drop in on friends to say hello—unannounced (choosing friends who are likely to appreciate the spontaneity, of course).
- Start or join a club—a book club, knitting club, cooking club, Scrabble club. Whatever your family's interests, you can start or join a club that celebrates it: theater, community service, wilderness camping, and much more.
- Get together with friends. This may sound simple, but just spending time with people we care about—or people we'd like to get to know—is a soul-satisfying kind of fun that is often a rarity in our harried lives. Throw something on the grill and have everyone bring a side dish. Or simply serve cookies and coffee. Or sit around the fireplace or the wading pool. Just hang out together.

Many of these simple things may seem a little unconventional now—even radical—although they weren't in our parents', or perhaps grandparents', time. I often think the most revolutionary thing we can do is just slow down, watch time pass together, and now and then enjoy some guilt-free daydreaming!

## FOR FURTHER READING

*Good Times Made Simple: The Lost Art of Fun,* the Center for a New American Dream, 6930 Carroll Avenue, Suite 900, Takoma Park, MD 20912, 1-877-68-DREAM, www.newdream.org

(A hefty pamphlet with creative ideas for having fun without spending a dime.)

*Fun Time, Family Time,* Susan K. Perry. New York, Avon Publishing, 1996.

*Just Family Nights,* edited by Susan Vogt. Elgin, IL, Brethren Press, 1994.

## ADDITIONAL RESOURCES

*Theatre for Young Adults, 20 Great Plays for Children,* Coleman Jennings. New York, St. Martin's Press, 1998.
(A book of plays that children can produce or enjoy viewing.)

*The Round Book—Rounds Kids Love to Sing,* Margaret Read MacDonald and Winifred Jaeger. North Haven, CT, Linnet Books, a division of The Shoe String Press, 1999.
(Easy songs for children and adults.)

*Creative Kids,* P.O. Box 8813, Waco, TX 76714, www.prufrock.com
(A noncommercial magazine of children's poetry, art, and essays for and by kids.)

*Babybug, Ladybug, Spider,* and *Cricket* Magazines, Cricket Publishing, P.O. Box 7433, Red Oak, IA 51591, 1-800-827-0227, www.cricketmag.com
(A noncommercial series of entertaining stories, activities, and resources for children, geared for the preschool child up to late middle school.)

*Cobblestone,* Caris Publishing, P.O. Box 300, Peru, IL 61354, 603-924-7209, www.cobblestonepub.com
(A noncommercial kids' magazine on American history for ages six through twelve.)

*Music for Little People,* P.O. Box 1460, Redway, CA 95560
(Great source of musical tapes for young children. Write for a catalog.)

*Mr. Beethoven Lives Upstairs,* produced by Margaret Levine Young and Jordon Young. Available on tape, CD, or video: 1-888-KID-TAPES or www.greattapes.com
(Excellent introduction to classical music for children ages six through ten.)

*Chinaberry,* www.chinaberry.com
(An online catalog of books for the whole family.)

# Chapter 13

# Happy, Healthy Holidays
# and Celebrations

*"Maybe Christmas," he [the Grinch] thought, "doesn't come from*
*a store. Maybe Christmas perhaps means a little bit more!"*
—from *How the Grinch Stole*
*Christmas* by Dr. Seuss

HOLIDAYS AND CELEBRATIONS are some of the most wonderful parts
of life. They used to be centered around religious observances (Easter,
Passover), life events and rites of passage (baptism, bar mitzvah), and
seasonal changes (the harvest, the equinox). More recently, commercial forces have taken hold. We gear up several times a year for special
holidays, but we are losing touch with any underlying meaning in the
midst of all the sales pitches. Try asking your kids, your friends, and
yourself what exactly you are celebrating on Labor Day, for example.
Nearly every significant national or family holiday has become an
obligation to spend money, and in the process we often forget what
our special commemorative days are honoring.

Take Halloween, for example. The ancient pleasure of mas-
querading in homemade masks and costumes has become a commercial event producing nearly $7 billion in annual sales, more than two
and a half times the estimated Halloween spending just five years ago.

The joy of assembling a completely novel costume has been overpowered by pressures to purchase upscale costumes of popular Disney and mass media celebrities ($1.5 billion a year). Add in the candy (at the rate of $1.93 billion in sales each year—more than Easter, Valentine's Day, or Christmas—fully one quarter of all the candy sold in a year), greeting cards ($50 million), and decorations and other thematic paraphernalia ($2.5 billion a year), and you've got a retail bonanza. But you've lost a little childhood magic.

I've faced this with my own family. When my son and daughter were younger, we made lots of wonderful costumes without spending a dollar. But each year, fewer and fewer friends joined in the fun, and more of their peers opted for prepackaged, expensive costumes mass-produced to emulate Hollywood characters. Some of their friends thought it just plain weird to assemble homemade costumes.

Many families are actively taking back the holidays. They are putting the "silent night" back into Christmas, or reclaiming Hanukkah without trying to mimic the consumerism that dominates Christmas. There's a whole movement of parents planning great birthday parties—without elaborate goody bags, expensive entertainers, or prepackaged chain store festivities. It's really possible to feel gratitude at Thanksgiving, spiritual renewal at Easter and Passover, and adventure at Halloween without spending money to acquire holiday *stuff.*

Your kids will thank you when you shift the focus from what they will *get* to what they will *do.* Really. It is often the adults, not the kids, who are the driving force behind elaborate and expensive celebrations.

Many adults would say that holidays—especially Christmas and birthdays—are more exhausting than uplifting. Often even kids feel let down, despite their eager anticipation. Grown-ups feel trapped by the frenzied preparations—shopping, spending (averaging upwards of $900 a year on Christmas gifts alone), planning, cooking, and cleaning—but yearn for a more meaningful observance. That's why one national survey showed that 70 percent of Americans would welcome less emphasis on gift giving and spending as part of the Christmas and Hanukkah holidays. These families don't want to rack up credit card debt (which studies show takes an average of six months to pay off after Christmas) or be slaves to seasonal commercialism.

This chapter focuses on how to simplify the holidays—whether the winter Christmas/Hanukkah extravaganza or any of the other overly commercialized corners of the calendar, including birthdays, Halloween, Valentine's Day, and major federal holidays. Every family will want to celebrate in its own way, depending on the occasion, but this chapter aims to help get you started down a new path, with steps to reduce stress and increase personal fulfillment during all the holidays. Most important, it includes ways to awaken your children to creating and treasuring new, less materialistic traditions. You won't be taking away from the holidays; you'll be restoring the meaning—and magic.

## WHAT DO YOU WANT FROM THE HOLIDAYS?

When we look back at our childhoods, holidays are often some of our most precious memories. What holiday memories are your children storing away now? What do you want them to remember? What will they remember twenty years from now? Does your usual celebration focus on the aspects of each holiday that you feel are most important? Picture the day after. The food is gone, the gifts have all been opened, you are collapsed on the couch. Imagine how the house looks, the way your family members are interacting, the way you feel. Is your image one of a happy afterglow? Letdown? Burnout?

Are the things you are doing to celebrate actually making the holiday joyful for you and yours? Which activities could you scale back on to reduce stress? Which can you get help with to make it easier on you and more enjoyable for everyone? Which activities truly enrich you and deserve more time and effort? How might we all recapture the true meaning of Memorial Day, Christmas, or Labor Day?

## SIMPLE GIFTS

One step in avoiding an annual shopping extravaganza and frenzied preparations for the picture-perfect holiday is to simplify your gift giving. You may be surprised to find that children are not the ones who put up the strongest arguments for a more lavish holiday.

There *is* some magic in gathering by the tree to open gifts. Gift giving is a wonderful thing and should not be abandoned—just modified. We all know that many families moan about their children's preoccupation with what and how much they will "get" from Santa Claus, rather than their focus on either the religious meaning of the holiday or the possibilities for family renewal and fun.

One key strategy for changing this is to substitute heartfelt experiences for mountains of material gifts. Give your kids some holiday experiences—ice skating on a real pond, storytelling by candlelight, or gatherings with cousins and friends to make the holidays truly memorable.

You might consider cutting back on the quantities of holiday gifts and instituting gift exchanges so that everyone doesn't buy for everyone else. You can try putting more meaning into the gifts you give. Don't deny your kids store-bought gifts, for surely some of these are fun and educational. But also consider giving your child a certificate for a whole day of your time, redeemable on two weeks' notice, for a trip to the local ballpark, museum, or roller rink. Or make them a gift such as painted wooden blocks, a backyard treehouse, or an audiotape about your family's history. Depending on your children's ages and interests, there are endless possibilities for homemade gifts; gifts of time; and gifts of your experience, talent, or expertise. Equally important, involve your kids with meaningful gift giving. Rather than rushing to buy something for every cousin and friend, encourage them to make homemade gifts.

For some people, the major stress of holiday time comes from entertaining. Starting in early October we are bombarded with images of designer Christmas decorations and elaborate holiday feasts. With these outsized requirements, a simple holiday party becomes a monstrous task. Consider simplifying this year, with support from your family. Instead of having a party centered around an extravagant meal, consider a gourmet potluck or have your kids help make a fancy dessert and just gather for coffee and cookies. Delegate decorating to your children and enjoy their homemade art. You really don't have to be like Martha Stewart.

Most important though is to instill meaning and magic into the Christmas, Hanukkah, Kwaanza, and other holiday seasons. What special childhood memories do you have that you might pass on to your kids? Consider going caroling, making a gingerbread house, or involving your children in charity for those who are less privileged. Invite someone you know would otherwise be alone to join you for your holiday meal. Megge, in Oregon, combines several of these ideas with her family each year: "With the kids, we go caroling with our neighbors at the retirement home down the block and in our neighborhood and then have a potluck at someone's house. We make cookies, put up our holiday village scene, and generally have a gay old time. Shopping is not big on anyone's list of things to do, so I did most of it early, on the Internet."

As Bill McKibben, environmentalist and author of *Hundred Dollar Holiday,* pointed out, "The most subversive thing to do is have more fun than other people. To the extent that your celebrations are more joyful, it may rub off a bit." This is especially true for children. "If you can make the holiday joyful enough," he said, "with enough points of real pleasure, parties, hikes, special activities, spending time together . . . the focus won't be so single-mindedly on how big the pile under the tree is."

Bill McKibben has his own favorite Christmas tradition: bringing birdseed and bread into the woods or a park and scattering it for the birds. "It's an old tradition of St. Francis, who said that animals deserve to celebrate this joyful thing . . . with a day when they have access to food. It's a wonderful way to remind yourself that this day is about a lot more than you and your desires."

## HAPPY BIRTHDAY TO YOU

Unfortunately, birthdays have taken on a lot of the same trappings as Christmas, and many parents feel distressed over the steady ratcheting up of the cost of birthday parties. But just like any other holidays, birthday celebrations too can focus more on fun and less on stuff. A little focus on the actual meaning of the occasion—the passage of one more year; the additional maturity, responsibility, and opportunity that brings; and the potential for new growth and adventure—helps too.

Help your kids focus more on what they are going to do rather than on what they are going to get. With a little tuning in to your child, and a bit of planning ahead, you can make the day as special as the child. Think interaction, adventure, challenge, fun. Here are some more specific ideas to get you started:

- Choose a theme carefully. Don't confuse themes with product placements. Go with princesses over Barbie, the color blue over *Blue's Clues,* ABCs and 123s over *Sesame Street.* Better still, try arts and crafts, drama, construction sites, or whatever gets the guest of honor excited.
- Omit the goody bags. Send your guests home with tales of an exciting experience instead, or perhaps a souvenir they made themselves as part of the fun (my kids have come home with hand-painted T-shirts, homemade jewelry, and picture frames with photos, to their great delight). If you simply must send guests home with something, try making wholesome goody bags with healthy snacks and homemade cookies, or provide a simple favor like a bag of popcorn tied with a fancy bow.
- Skip the ready-made parties offered by chain stores and create your own traditions instead, reflecting your deeper values—and the personality of your child. Instead of spending a small fortune for pizza and video games at a cheesy restaurant, for example, organize your own pizza party at home (perhaps letting the kids make their own).

- Have fun with your choice of refreshments. Add a creative spark by letting every child decorate her own cupcake, or skip the cake altogether and serve make-your-own sundaes instead. Or try something completely different. Create a picnic. Make chocolate fondue. Have a bake-off, with each guest bringing a dessert (perhaps instead of a gift) for everyone to taste.
- Play up your child's growing ability to do new things by granting a new experience: Finally, they are old enough to camp out overnight, handle their own canoe, have a rock-music party, or go to the movies on the bus by themselves.
- Center a party around old-fashioned games such as relay races, balancing a potato on a spoon, three-legged or wheelbarrow races, bobbing for apples, tossing water balloons from one child to another, or eating donuts suspended on strings from the ceiling (no hands allowed!).
- Teenagers might consider having a dance party, coed softball game, or spending an evening playing board games such as Balderdash or Taboo.
- For young kids, keep it simple. Don't invite the whole class (go with parenting experts' common recommendation: one guest for each candle on the cake). Get out the dress-up box, or a collection of musical instruments, or a felt storyboard, or art supplies.
- Dictionary, charades, and skits are fun and can help the group get over initial shyness.
- If your family has a video camera, the kids can make a homemade film or documentary, or record a homemade play. Have each guest bring some dress-up clothes and silly props, and let their imaginations run wild.
- Have a costume party with everyone coming dressed from a different time period, in a particular color, or representing their favorite Harry Potter or literary character.

Go back to basics to discover the magic that will truly get your child jazzed.

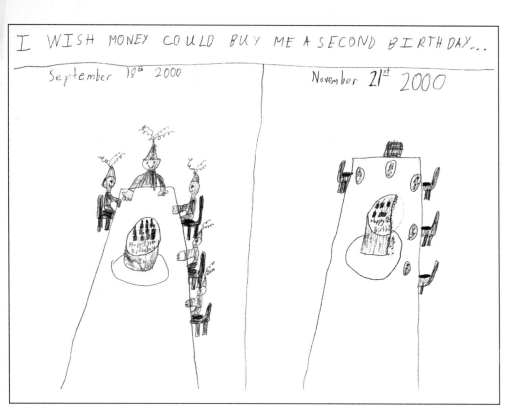

"I wish money could buy me a second birthday..." Artist: Mike S.

## ALTERNATIVE GIFT GIVING

It's troubling that both birthdays and Christmas in the United States are increasingly all about volume. American toymakers issue between three and six thousand new toys every year. In the 1980s, the average preschooler asked for three or four toys at holiday time—and received eleven or twelve. In 1994, $1.2 *billion* was spent on Barbie dolls alone—at a time when the average girl already owned eight Barbies.

But it doesn't have to be like that. Lynn Deed of Maryland wrote in to the Center about her approach to birthdays: "Probably the most innovative thing I have done is to have 'no present' birthday parties.

We started this early in their childhood, so there really hasn't been any problem. The boys know that's just the way it is, and I think that they realize they don't need the extra stuff. Some of the responses from parents have been interesting. I usually get a questioning call, and we occasionally get 'nonpresents' such as home-baked cookies, used books, etc." Of course, many families won't want to eliminate gifts completely, but you might consider some alternative gift-giving approaches.

The following sections of this chapter catalog a host of unconventional gift ideas that you might consider in your family. Again, it doesn't mean denying your children a super skateboard or a fashionable outfit. It does mean bringing your full attention to the range of possibilities and putting an emphasis on magic, not material goods. When 82 percent of Americans say they would much rather receive a photo album documenting shared times than a store-bought gift (according to a poll by my organization), you know you can't go wrong with personalized, heartfelt gifts. Kathy, a parent who lives in Maryland, has several creative approaches: "Our kids made, rather than bought, presents for their immediate family and cousins, and some of the presents were 'recycled' (e.g., my daughter passed on to her younger cousin a complete set of the previous year's *Ladybug* magazines). We also gave presents of tickets or coupons (e.g., theater tickets for adults, and coupons for special one-on-one meals out for teenagers), instead of manufactured objects, to several family members."

## Gifts of Time

This is a wonderful option for just about anyone, from the friends who have "everything" to elderly relatives who would most appreciate your companionship. Draw up a coupon or certificate proclaiming that it entitles the bearer to whatever you are promising. Include a loving message about why you are honoring this person, give instructions for redeeming it if necessary, and decorate to your heart's desire. These are gifts that can be given to children or by children. Both giving and receiving gifts of time can add meaning to any holiday event. Here are a few examples, some appropriate for kids to receive and some more appropriate for them to give:

- A favorite meal prepared for no special occasion other than celebrating the recipient
- A month of taking out the garbage or doing the dishes or some other household chore
- A monthly lunch date
- Ten back rubs
- A pledge to keep one's bedroom picked up for one solid month
- A certain number of hours or days of baby-sitting
- Homemade meals delivered to the recipient's house—or pre-pared and served (and cleaned up) in the home of the receiver
- Five car washes
- A handwritten letter sent once a month for a year
- A day of hiking, or a picnic
- Fifteen rounds of your child's favorite game
- A day off from school with Mom or Dad doing something really special

## Gifts of Experience

This kind of gift can provide memories that last forever—or at least a lot longer than just another toy. Give someone a new or exciting experience. (One year, our whole family—aunts, uncles, cousins, grand-parents—went go-cart riding. We ended up in tears, we were laughing so hard.) Or share your experience or expertise.

- Offer to teach your kids a skill you possess, such as fishing, building furniture, doing the butterfly stroke, baking bread, throwing a fast ball, growing tomatoes, taking great photos, or playing a song on the guitar.
- Go to a zoo, aquarium, or local historical site.

- Go camping, rent canoes, or arrange an all-day bike trip.
- Offer to use one of your skills on your child's behalf, such as analyzing the stock market, sewing bedroom curtains, doing her hair before a big night out, or building a bookcase.
- Go swimming, ice skating, bowling, or inline skating.
- Take a train ride.
- Climb a mountain.
- Visit an archeological dig.
- Find a pen pal.

Carol, a California woman, wrote to the Center about her favorite gift to give: "I like to give dramatic, unusual experiences, not stuff, for gifts. For example, I traditionally take my nephew camping or create a treasure hunt for his birthday. For the treasure hunt, I make up rhyming clues to challenge him and head him off in all directions. I started this when he first learned to read, with clues leading him around his house to a small gift. Now, at thirteen, his clues take him all through our downtown and require him to interact with other people in funny scenarios. I overheard him telling a friend how cool a treasure hunt is. The friend said, 'Wow, there must be a really big present at the end.' Then he said, 'No, the present is the hunt!'"

## Homemade Gifts

You do not have to be an artist, or even exceptionally creative, to make a great gift for someone. And while it does take some time to make a gift, it may be no more than the time you spend hunting for a parking spot at the mall! You can't go wrong with a basket of home-made baked goods, for example, but with a little imagination your options are many and varied. To take just one example, a Maryland mom named Lila shared her favorite gifts with the Center: "We'll bring down one or two old, small branches from our cedar trees and make cedar blocks for friends' drawers, and we'll give a coupon to our neighbor for one spring tilling of her garden." To inspire you, more ideas follow:

- Make an audio- or videotape of family and friends discussing their memories of the recipient, including especially funny or meaningful anecdotes.
- Create a web page featuring the receiver.
- Put together a collection of favorite family recipes, or your tried-and-true favorites, or a collection of recipes with a theme tailored to the recipient—vegetarian food, chocolate, breads and pastries, recipes simple enough for kids to make, and so on.
- Tape older family members giving the family history, reminiscing about childhood, describing life at different time periods, and sharing their life lessons, to give not only to them, but to their descendants as well.
- Make a calendar decorated with photos; drawings; collages; favorite quotations; or personalized daily, weekly, or monthly messages. Don't forget to mark important dates such as birthdays, anniversaries, and family reunions.
- Put together pictures and mementos in a photo album, scrapbook, framed collage, or storyboard poster centered around a certain person or family, specific event, time period, or theme.
- Record your child playing an instrument.
- List one hundred of your fondest memories of the recipient.
- Give bulbs or cuttings from house and garden plants.
- Give a birdseed ball made of seed and suet for hanging outside.

## Charitable Gifts

The dominant holiday culture encourages everyone to focus on getting gifts, for our kids and us. But many holidays, especially religious ones, have deeper meaning about transcendence and a relationship with the sacred. These occasions offer special opportunities for giving to charity. Include your children in charitable giving and help build a lifelong connection and compassion for those who may be living with unmet material and human needs.

- Donate to a cause in someone's name. Consider sponsoring a child refugee, protecting an acre of rain forest, or buying a certain number of blankets for a homeless shelter. Getting specific helps make it more meaningful, especially for children. Making it local can also make it more special to the person you are honoring with the donation. Think of a way to honor something particular about a person: Donate books to a library in honor of your favorite bookworm, or support a hospital in honor of an aspiring doctor, or give equipment to an inner-city sports team on behalf of your Little Leaguer.
- Be a "Secret Santa." Some post offices, YMCAs, and other groups and organizations run programs at holiday time in which volunteers pick a child's name and "wish," buy the gift, and wrap it up for the sponsoring group to deliver.
- Have a tree planted in someone's honor.
- Give a membership in a nonprofit organization that works in an area the recipient is particularly interested in.
- "Adopt" an animal through a wildlife organization.

### Simple, Environmentally Friendly Gifts

When you are buying a more traditional type of gift, avoid fads and poorly made or plastic goods in favor of gifts that will last—both because they are durable and because they are timeless. Choose gifts that will encourage family time together, time in nature, and creative use of free time—the ends you're aiming for in this book. Try to avoid packaging and plastic. (I'm thrilled that one major toy maker has promised to produce some biodegradable toys that are nontoxic and environmentally friendly. Let's hope they deliver on that promise soon.) Often, the less complicated a gift is, the more it engages a child's imagination. When you are buying, support local businesses and artisans when you can. "Buying local" is good for the environment and the local community. Consider timeless toys such as these:

- Jigsaw puzzle
- Camping equipment
- Gift certificate to a local new or used bookstore
- Bag of marbles
- Foreign coins or stamps
- Magnifying glass
- Art/craft supplies
- Building blocks
- Modeling clay or homemade play dough
- A journal or interesting paper with special pens
- Photo album to fill
- Musical instruments
- Stationery (100 percent recycled with soy-based ink!)

## Adventure in a Box

Fun is often right in front of us if we simply gather a few household items and reinvent them as toys or props for "pretend play." Gather the materials that a young child can use to make a whole imaginary world. Often you can do this out of things you already have on hand, or that won't cost anything. Assembled properly in fun combinations with a bunch of other things, these kits can be better than anything you can buy in a store.

- Empty food boxes, play money, and a cash box for running a store
- Old checks, business forms, carbon paper, rubber stamps, and file folders to play office
- Scrap wood, shingles, a hammer, and nontoxic paint for building a clubhouse—and a map that shows where it can be

built. For younger children, get your hands on an empty refrigerator box, cut out a door and a window or two, and let them decorate their hideout.

- Old nightgowns, shirts, jackets, wild shoes, silly ties and hats, and costume jewelry for playing dress-up
- Gardening tools and seeds—with their own plot to plant, or pots of soil for indoor gardening
- The makings for hand puppets—brown lunch bags, old socks, googly eyes, feathers, yarn, buttons, and glue
- A friend of mine created for her young niece a gift of a jewelry box filled with all kinds of inexpensive costume jewelry. It was a big hit.

## Beyond Gifts

Just remember, in the end, holidays are not primarily about gifts. Now and then consider celebrating Labor Day by remembering the workers in your family's history rather than going to the mall; celebrate Memorial Day with a visit to your local veterans memorial or cemetery, remembering soldiers who bravely gave their lives for our freedom; celebrate the Fourth of July by making a float in the local parade rather than rushing to the preholiday retail sales; honor President's Day not with a new online order but with an evening of prose written by Lincoln, Jefferson, Kennedy, and your own favorite presidents. Think about the meaning of our holidays, and reclaim special traditions that we've lost to Madison Avenue.

## FOR FURTHER READING

*Simplify the Holidays,* a pamphlet available from the Center for a New American Dream, 6930 Carroll Avenue, Suite 900, Takoma Park, MD 20912, www.newdream.org

*One Hundred Dollar Holiday: The Case for a Joyful Christmas,* Bill McKibben. Riverside, NJ, Simon & Schuster, 1998.
(A lovely book about alternative approaches to celebrating Christmas.)

*The Heart of a Family: Searching America for New Traditions that Fulfill Us,*
  Meg Cox. New York, Random House Publishing, 1998.
  (Ideas for reclaiming or starting new, meaningful traditions in the home.)

## OTHER RESOURCES

Alternative Gifts, P.O. Box 2267, Lucerne Valley, CA 92356, 1-800-842-2243,
  www.altgifts.org
  (Alternative Gifts International allows you to give gifts to charities around
  the world in the name of a friend or family member.)
American Forests, P.O. Box 2000, Washington, DC 20013, 1-202-955-4500,
  www.americanforests.org
  (You can have a tree planted in someone's honor through American
  Forests.)
Heifer Project International, P.O. Box 8058, Little Rock, AR 72203, 1-800-
  422-0474, www.heifer.org
  (The Heifer Project helps you donate agricultural equipment and small ani-
  mals to support peasants in developing countries.)

# Chapter 14

# What Do YOU Want
# That Money Can't Buy?

LIVING WELL can be a challenge. It certainly is for me. Many of us hope that life will eventually settle down, but it never quite does. Change, for better or worse, is inevitable. We often spend our time grasping for something we can't quite put our fingers on and seldom reflect on what we *really* want. This chapter is an invitation to pause, put your feet up, and think about how you too can recapture those precious things in life that money can never buy.

I'm sure I'm not the only adult who recognizes many of my own wants in the dreams and hopes of children. Adults too want friends, respect, more time, good health, and fun. We need and want financial security, but we also yearn for more soul-satisfying experiences and ways of being. The desire for discovering some other way to live, beyond the "work-rush-spend-do" definition of the good life, is strong. In a 1995 poll conducted by the Harwood Group, 66 percent of American adults said they would be much more satisfied with life, if they were able to spend more time with family and friends. How can we stay connected to our authentic needs and experience greater contentment?

## THE HIDDEN COSTS OF THE "MORE IS BETTER" AMERICAN DREAM

The traditional American dream once focused on greater security, opportunity, and happiness. Increasingly, that dream has been supplanted by a highly commercial culture. More is never enough. This race is fueled by fear of an uncertain future, individualism gone to extremes, and lifestyles defined by acquisition. From bigger houses and SUVs to large-screen TVs and supersized food portions, our appetites keep expanding. But are we happier? Nearly three fourths of those polled by the Harwood Group said they had more possessions than their parents had at the same age, yet less than half said they were happier than their parents. Maybe the lack of contentment is connected to our heavy work and debt loads. The average employed American now works more than forty-seven hours a week in the struggle to keep up. One study shows that Americans put in more time on the job in the year 2000 than did workers in any other industrialized nation. At the same time, millions of Americans have racked up so much debt that the national savings rate has plunged to historic lows while personal bankruptcy rates have skyrocketed.

We need to make some choices, as individuals and as a society. And so far we haven't necessarily made the right ones. According to Juliet Schor, author of *The Overworked American,* "We could now reproduce our 1948 standard of living (measured in terms of marketed goods and services) in less than half the time it took in 1948. We actually could have chosen the four-hour day. Or a working year of six months. Or imagine this: Every worker in the United States could now be taking every other year off from work, with pay."

## WHAT DO WE REALLY WANT?

In a class I once taught for adults on alternatives to materialism and the consumer culture, I asked everyone to think about their true, authentic sources of happiness—and share them with the class. While a few were understandably material (one guy was rapturous about his great new toolbox and his ability to fix things), most were simple, free, and available to anyone who wanted them. One woman said she felt joyful when she had her cat in her lap, purring. Someone else felt bliss when dancing, and another felt peaceful when arranging flowers. The list went on like that: true friendship, solitude, music, sunshine, children, intimacy, the woods, satisfying work, good books, independence, travel, making a difference, laughter, prayer, really being heard, feeling loved. The Center for a New American Dream doesn't have to run a poll of adults to show that, in a happy coincidence, what grown-ups really want that money can't buy is pretty much the same as what kids want. Make your own list. What do *you* really want that money can't buy?

When you feel you're in a race in which everyone and everything is about to overtake you, it's helpful to stay tuned in to what you really care about. This chapter focuses on practices and priorities that can help you live a more balanced life and find more of that precious contentment so many of us crave.

## SLOW DOWN, MEDITATE, AND LISTEN

The number one prerequisite for knowing and meeting your deepest needs is to slow down enough to get in touch with your inner self. When we stay in motion and focus externally, we are bombarded with messages and images intended to shape our wants and preferences. According to *Business Week,* the average American adult receives over three thousand commercial messages a day. Our authentic desires are reawakened when we slow down and turn inward. There are several ways to do this—some simple and some more challenging. When we're preoccupied with worries and mental lists of things that must get done, we're too overloaded to really know where we are or where we want to be.

You can start by simply being conscious of the desire to slow down and resist the speed of life. We all have little tricks for doing this. When you are rushed, stuck in traffic, anxious about a deadline, or racing to a soccer practice, try to be fully present in the moment and let go of any tension you're feeling. The Buddhists call this mindfulness, and at its core it's about focusing our senses to appreciate the simple wonders of each moment. In the now, you can let your worries go.

Consider setting aside a small amount of time for silence, reflection, or quiet prayer. It often feels as though I can't spare one minute out of the 1,440 allotted per day. But I try, not always successfully, to create at least five minutes, and ideally more than twenty, when I literally just stop and exist in quietness—a time not of actively *doing,* but rather of just *being.* Meditation creates a space in which we can let go of our grasping and focus on the present—not the memories of yesterday or the anticipation of tomorrow, but on the present day, the immediate moment. One of the peculiar things about human beings is that we tend to put off living. We dream of some perfect place in the future, or worry about what might happen, instead of enjoying a bird's song, the presence of a friend, and other blessings available to us each and every moment. We won't always find insight or tranquility through this practice, but now and then it's possible to connect to a deeper ocean of calm and to feel part of something larger and more universal than the self.

## FOCUS ON FRIENDS

Seek out friends who share your values and interests and place a priority on these relationships. When we multitask and are on the go 24/7, it's hard to make time for friends. Yet our lives and communities are fragmented, and most of us need friends more than ever before. We all want friends—to inspire and energize us, to support us in tough times, and to laugh with. And fortunately, we don't need lots of friends to feel deeply satisfied. Stanford University psychology professor Laura Carstensen has studied friendships among older Americans and concludes, "It is the quality of their relationships that matters—

not the quantity." In her research, she found that three is the critical friend number. If you have three people in your life that you can really count on, then you are doing as well as someone who has ten friends.

Jan Yager, author of *Friendshifts,* says that making and maintaining friendships is really pivotal to social, emotional, and physical well-being, including our longevity. So take steps to reconnect and place a priority on close friends. Try carving out time for more walks, bike rides, phone calls, and visits with the handful of your closest friends whom you have come to really trust, care for, and enjoy being with. I know of a woman who holds a weekly "chop and chat" morning; she invites over friends to prepare their meals for the week ahead, and they talk as they cook. Also, it can be extremely rewarding to try to track down an old friend with whom you've lost touch—even if the person was a friend as far back as junior high or elementary school. Another idea is to have a weekend getaway with one of your best friends. One's friends can serve as an anchor when things go awry, and as a source of happiness in the good times.

Many of us focus on self-improvement, often with good cause. The desire to achieve, make an impact, and improve ourselves is a wonderful part of human nature, but sometimes we become slaves to our intense schedules and standards. When we spend more time cultivating relationships with others, we can transcend our restless need to do or be more. Try finding part of your sense of affirmation through relationships rather than achievements.

## REDUCE STRESS AND SCALE BACK

We all know that high stress contributes to a myriad of problems including alcoholism, overeating, and divorce. Life often feels like one permanent emergency, and when we rush all the time, we create the conditions for a breakdown. When your legs get heavy and tired, try to do less. Say *no* more often. Question the need to always stay one step ahead of the group—a sure cause of stress. And ask yourself if you're in a race in which nobody can really be a winner. Sometimes, by stepping back from the scramble, we gain perspective and realize that we really can do less, and in the end the world will go on just fine without our extra effort.

If possible, consider options for working and spending less. Maybe it means negotiating reduced working hours and postponing or skipping the bathroom makeover. According to several public opinion polls, millions of Americans are opting to work reduced hours, usually with a corresponding pay cut, in order to have more time for the things in life that really matter to them. This is obviously not an option for everyone, either financially or for other practical reasons (such as low wages or a completely inflexible workplace). But a number of government agencies, private companies, and nonprofit organizations are experimenting with flexible work arrangements that help employees reduce stress and recapture time for other parts of life.

Part of reducing stress involves reorienting our state of mind. We worry and struggle to control the outcomes of our efforts, at work and home. And of course, sometimes we have to. Lower-income families especially carry heavy stress that stems from real fears about meeting core survival needs. Sometimes, though, when the stakes aren't really so high, we can reduce stress by doing our best and then letting go of the consequences.

## LET TECHNOLOGY ENHANCE, NOT RUN, YOUR LIFE

We live with the web, satellite and cable TV, cell phones, the Ethernet, DVDs, Palm Pilots, and electronic mail. Most of these technologies weren't around in a significant way ten years ago, but now virtual environments are everywhere. And while online communities and digital effects have their place, many people complain that things are spinning out of control. Nobody can keep up with all the incoming stimuli, information, and choices. As human beings we do have limits on how much we can absorb, how fast we can process, and how much we can keep under control.

Eventually there may be a retreat from the overload of our electronic information revolution, but in the meantime we're all in the thick of it. The challenge is to harness technology for better living rather than be saddled with an unprecedented amount of electronic entertainment and information.

Consider the following options:

- Watch less television and plant more flowers.
- Give up your cell phone or use it only for true emergencies, and spend time in the cracks of your schedule slowing down instead of doing more.
- Go off e-mail for at least one month a year to recapture that time for conversation, reading, or a personal hobby. People will understand, especially if we all start doing it!
- Resist upgrading just because you can.
- Resist the latest gadget—such as the newest model of digital electronic organizer—especially if you foresee that it will dominate your free time and take you away from your family (and it probably will!).
- Spend at least one week each year giving up all electronic entertainment, radio, and newspapers. Consider having an adventure, exploring a state park, inviting neighbors over for charades, or building a tree house. Rebel against the system.
- Watch one less video and enjoy one more sunset.
- Don't answer the phone during dinnertime. Make this a time for slowing down and reconnecting with your family.

## SEEK REGULAR CONTACT WITH NATURE

This takes conscious effort if you live in a more urban, congested area, with days spent commuting, working in artificial light and indoor air, and evenings often spent recovering in front of the television. But most of us slow down and gain perspective by spending time in nature. It doesn't have to be some great backwoods adventure. Try just taking a walk outside several times a week, and spend it being really attentive to the beauty. You may often find your mind spinning with all you have to do, but try to be mindful and gently refocus, over and over again if necessary, in favor of looking at the clouds and trees, feeling the wind, or smelling some blossoms. Invite a colleague to take a walk during your lunch break and just let go of that whole list of details and small worries we all carry around in our heads, at least temporarily, and find your way back to what is important. It can literally be a breath of fresh air.

Try one or more of these suggestions:

- Take lunch outside at a nearby park once a week.
- Make a habit of taking your children outside to look at the stars before bedtime.
- Get to know your own place and enjoy exploring the local ecosystem in your area.
- Get up to watch the sunrise several times a year.
- Meet your spouse for a picnic in a beautiful spot.
- Go camping.
- Get out of the suburbs or inner city at least a few times a year to climb a mountain, canoe a lake, or hike a quiet trail.

## REBEL, HAVE FUN, AND PLAY

Rebel against your schedule. We are consistently rewarded for hard work and multitasking. But we're out of touch with our senses, and we're often too tired to feel playful. Rediscover fun. Once in a while, we all need to put aside our to-do lists, shut out all the demands on us, and act on our deeper desires. Take some time out for an adventure. Dance, take a fishing trip, or plan a weekend away with friends. What is fun for you? Build something. Paint. Go rock climbing. Spend a day at the beach. Go visit your grandmother and tape her stories. Plant something. Get curious about anything—a Civil War battle or an architectural style. Feeling alive is directly connected to staying curious. Surprise someone by phoning him or her out of the blue. Bake bread. Linger in a library. Play an instrument. Don't just talk about it or dream about it—do it!

My kids recently had a half day of school. I'd gotten back the day before from an extended business trip and had absolutely no time to do anything but catch up at the office. Nonetheless, we took off and played for the day. First we had our favorite French toast breakfast, eaten at a leisurely pace. Then we took off on bikes to a nearby park. Later we settled in for a few lively board games, including Boggle and Scrabble. Toward the end of the day, I slipped away for a hot bath by candlelight and later had a glass of wine with my husband while the kids just hung out, read books, organized their bedrooms, did some planning for long-term school projects, and later waited for me to tuck them in to bed. It was a nice respite from the daily rush— for all of us. I found I really could take the day off, and the office would get along without me. I caught up the next day, perhaps not answering every e-mail, but knowing that my priorities were in the right place. And by playing hooky for a day, I was far more refreshed and energized for work than I would have been if I had rushed in and tried to run on empty. Sometimes we just have to say no to the regular routine and expectations of others and grab the immediate joys of life.

## PURSUE WISDOM

Most of us seek out books to help us along our path. Make time for poetry, novels, and sacred texts that help you stay connected to your values and dreams. Besides the comfort and inspiration you can find, reading is one way of staying in community, including being tied to a historical network of humans who together have been searching for the good life. From old and new, there is so much to learn. Check out the books and resources listed at the end of each chapter of this book. Many people spend ten minutes each morning reading from books of short psalms, poems, or prayers and combine these readings with a short period of prayer or meditation before they hit the rush of the day. I know of a married couple who read out loud to each other every night before going to sleep—a lovely ritual. There is wisdom in the past, and in many of our fellow travelers asking the same questions.

Consider keeping a journal, either as a meditative practice, a spiritual or psychological exercise, or just to make your thinking concrete. It doesn't have to be daily to be valuable. I go to my journal about once a week, sometimes more often, sometimes less. I track where I am, note my ups and downs, and reflect on new insights or obstacles. I often jot down notes from books or articles that give me new ways of understanding or write about events that have influenced my daily life. I periodically return and make a list of what I most want in life and note if I'm generally achieving the balance and connections that are most important to me. Many people find this practice helpful.

Never stop pondering life's larger questions: What is really important? How much is enough? What do I really want and need? What is my connection or obligation to people who are needlessly suffering? Probe for ways of living that reflect your positive values: Why am I rushing? What can I do to stay fully alive and in touch with my deepest values, wants, and needs? What makes me happy? How can I stay centered in a world that is out of balance? When do I feel truly peaceful? Am I helping make the world a better place? Am I having fun yet? What do *I* want that money can't buy?

Talk about these questions with your spouse, as well as your kids. These are not issues we settle once and for all. In fact, if all goes well, we'll probably be asking them of ourselves our whole life long. But when we live the questions, as the poet Rilke urged us to do, we stay alive to our own hearts—and tune out the dominant, pulsating culture that constantly urges us to buy our way to fulfillment.

## HELP CHANGE THE SYSTEM

Many people who ask the question, What do I really want that money can't buy? are also interested in how to change the system. How do we create a society that helps everyone stay connected to what really matters in life? We cannot avoid these bigger questions. They rest in the depths of this book. The personal challenge is in the quest for balance. The political challenge is engaging enough of us to do our small part so that together we can actually change the system.

We need to restructure things, sooner rather than later. Why can't we convert our world-class productivity into a world-class society that supports families? In other words, let's push for a four-day workweek—something that President Nixon predicted would come to pass long ago. Let's stand up and say no to marketing and advertising to young children. They've done it in Canada. They've done it in Germany and Sweden. If they can do it, why can't we? Stop acquiescing to the sanctification of the market above all else and insist that society is meant for more than just private enterprise. It is meant for people, and people need to be cared for. We need a safety net to allow people to slow down and care for their kids. The United States stands alone among the world's top industrialized nations as the single country that does not provide universal health care for its citizens. Nor does it guarantee any help with many other core basic needs, unlike its European and Canadian counterparts. We can debate the details of the necessary solutions, but the bottom line is that more families need health care, better public schools, affordable housing, and more tax breaks for retirement savings if they hope to slow down and ease the fear in their hearts. Without more societal support for these collective needs, it's every family for itself, and the pressure to keep up will remain intense.

## BEYOND THE SELF

All the sacred traditions suggest that true contentment involves letting go—of pain, loss, the need to control, and the grasping for more. It involves forgiveness, of yourself if you have knowingly or otherwise hurt someone, and of others who might have hurt you. It requires allegiance to something larger than the self. People everywhere celebrate lives lived in the service of a higher purpose or in dedication to others. They always have.

When we allow ourselves to be moved by a vision or a call to social action, public service, or care for others, it taps something deep within us. Often we resist at first, or avoid acting on our dreams due to fears, a sense of powerlessness, or the belief that heart-based work is impractical. Sadly, our dreams and gifts often get suppressed as time passes and our schedules become habitual. We take fewer risks and often have a hard time imagining how to transcend the constraints of what seems possible, both personally and for society as a whole. But when we opt to act out of a place of empathy and love, wonderful things usually happen. When we start jumping off the (metaphorical) cliff, following our dreams, and listening to our inner voices, we often go through a radical inner transformation that makes us see the world differently.

There are many ways of finding your own special role and of using your unique gifts for making the world a better place. It helps to quiet down and get centered. I've found it helpful also to be in relationship with someone who lives on the economic margins of our society. These kinds of friendships can be transformative and clear the cobwebs when it comes to figuring out what's important and answering the question, How much is enough? So slow down, listen, and notice if there is a pull on your heart to serve or help tackle a problem on behalf of the common good. Maybe it just involves showing a little kindness to someone who is ignored at the office, or perhaps you're meant to visit with an elderly friend.

Often, when we go deep and get quiet, we feel a tug. It's not always immediate, and it can take time to distinguish between a genuine calling and a mere fantasy, but try simply listening to your own inner voice. Is there something you've always wished you could do, but it just didn't seem practical? Perhaps you have wanted to change something at your office or blow the whistle on a bad practice. Maybe you're meant to start a service project with fellow workers, or perhaps you're supposed to do even more. Some people leave their jobs to teach, become social workers, bring business expertise to nonprofit groups, set up after-school programs for needy kids, go overseas with a foreign relief agency, or get involved politically. Every person has a gift and often a vision of something that could be better—some facet of life that needs changing. Whatever the heartfelt pull, pay attention. It's probably part of what you deeply want that money can never buy.

## TRANSCENDING FEAR

There is a lot of suppressed fear in our culture. Despite our extraordinary freedom and our nation's dominance on the world stage, many Americans don't feel safe. We fear what the future may bring, especially for our kids. We worry about being cared for in our old age. We fear being alone. Many now worry about terrorism, war, and the possibility of things just falling apart. We fear falling behind, and of course, many of us fear death. Some psychologists and sociologists argue that the primary driver behind our phenomenal race, chase, and incessant pursuit of more stems from our need to suppress our fears and worries. Perhaps one part of our journey must include the courageous attempt to face these fears and find hope in solutions such as community, friends, faith, and human compassion.

For some, working for long-term solutions such as health care and housing policies that provide everyone with greater security can mitigate fear. When we feel safe and protected in a community of mutually supportive families or in the experience of the sacred, we can let go of anxieties. When we help work for solutions to systemic problems and know that others are helping too, we feel less fear and more genuine hope. When we reconnect with nature, family, and simple pleasures, we are restored, and fear abates. By strengthening community and working for a strong social safety net, the fears may not entirely subside, but they definitely don't have to dominate our lives. By reclaiming the simple joys of conversation, outdoor exploration, friendship, and fun, we can find a sense of safety, ease, and release from worries about the future.

## IS LOVE THE ANSWER?

Maybe when all is said and done, humans are meant for love. Maybe it is deeply encoded in our DNA. I think so. I think we are absolutely programmed to give and receive it—that this is the core want of all children and adults. In the midst of tensions and anxieties about maintaining our lifestyles, or about anything else, we need to be living in the service of love. The antidote to our aloneness and our search for meaning is the possibility of love. This capacity for deep human connection, for sacred space and a sense of belonging to the whole natural world, is the fundamental answer to the question, What do I really want that money can't buy?

Love is the one thing that can overcome fear, insecurity, and pain. Unlike the competitive race for more as a tactic for maximizing

"…money can't buy…love from my family!!" Artist: Cindy

aliveness and happiness, love has more to do with opening our hearts and less to do with getting ahead. We must listen and stay in touch with something greater than ourselves, whether we call it God, the law of nature, the Tao, or our inner voice. From this place we rediscover our best intentions and a spirit of understanding and compassion. We can forgive. We can love anew, despite our broken past. From this place, we can feel deeply loved despite any shortcomings, and in return, can freely give love away. We will be motivated to spend more of our life energy in service to the common good, not from a sense of obligation but from an internal feeling of deep connection to other people.

So embrace love as the core organizing principle for life. It's what your kids really want that money can't buy. It's what *we* really want that money can't buy.

## FOR FURTHER READING

*The Art of Loving,* Erich Fromm. New York, Perrennial, a division of HarperCollins, 2000. First published London, Harper & Row, 1956.
*The Road Less Traveled: A New Psychology of Love, Traditional Values and Spiritual Growth,* Scott Peck. Buccaneer Books, 1995.

# Author's Note

The Center for a New American Dream is a nonprofit membership organization helping Americans consume responsibly to improve quality of life, protect the environment, and enhance social justice. It works with individuals, institutions, communities, and businesses to conserve natural resources, counter the commercialization of our culture, and reclaim the non-material joys of life.

The Center was founded in 1997. The stock market may have been at an all-time high then, but there seemed to be a simmering undercurrent that the "more is better" definition of the American dream had hidden costs—more work, more stress, disconnected families, less free time, and environmental degradation. Ms. Taylor helped start the Center for a New American Dream because she saw the need to foster a different dream, one based on stewardship of resources, mutual responsibility, material security, and a celebration of those nonmaterial parts of life that really matter. The Center is both visionary and practical; it seeks to facilitate both the dreaming and the doing. It helps individuals and institutions recognize the urgent need for change, not by pointing fingers, but by pointing out solutions. The Center believes firmly in the American "can-do" spirit and emphasizes a step-by-step approach to making a difference. The Center maintains a staff of twenty employees. Ms. Taylor and the Center's board and staff believe firmly that making the world a better place must include having a life that's full of fun and fulfillment along the way.

The Center's interactive and informative website, www.new-dream.org, receives more than one million visits (and thirty million hits) per year, and the organization produces a variety of printed resources full of practical suggestions for raising healthy kids, consuming wisely, and having more fun with less stuff. These include their extremely popular quarterly publication *Enough!*, as well as the pamphlets *Tips for Parenting in a Commercial Culture, Simplify the Holidays,* and *Good Times Made Simple: The Lost Art of Fun.*

Membership in the Center is $30 a year. Members receive a free copy of the *More Fun, Less Stuff Starter Kit,* a subscription to *Enough!,* and a More Fun, Less Stuff bumper or bike sticker. For more information, contact:

The Center for a New American Dream
6930 Carroll Avenue, Suite 900
Takoma Park, MD 20912
877-68-DREAM
www.newdream.org